Eudora at home, working in her bedroom, 1940s.

One Writer's Beginnings

Eudora Welty

SCRIBNER

New York   London   Toronto   Sydney   New Delhi

Scribner
An Imprint of Simon & Schuster, Inc.
1230 Avenue of the Americas
New York, NY 10020

This Scribner trade paperback edition November 2020

SCRIBNER and design are registered trademarks of The Gale Group, Inc., used under license by Simon & Schuster, Inc., the publisher of this work.

For information about special discounts for bulk purchases, please contact Simon & Schuster Special Sales at 1-866-506-1949 or business@simonandschuster.com.

The Simon & Schuster Speakers Bureau can bring authors to your live event. For more information, or to book an event, contact the Simon & Schuster Speakers Bureau at 1-866-248-3049 or visit our website at www.simonspeakers.com.

Manufactured in the United States of America

3   5   7   9   10   8   6   4   2

Library of Congress Cataloging-in-Publication Data has been applied for.

ISBN 978-1-9821-5177-5
ISBN 978-1-9821-5210-9 (pbk)
ISBN 978-1-9821-5298-7 (ebook)

To the memory of my parents

Christian Webb Welty
1879–1931

Chestina Andrews Welty
1883–1966

Contents

Introduction by Natasha Trethewey   ix

I

Listening   1

II

Learning to See   55

III

Finding a Voice   95

Acknowledgments   141

Introduction

For a long time I've kept a copy of Eudora Welty's *One Writer's Beginnings* close at hand, among the collection of books stacked on my desk. Though I swap them out as I move on to new projects, Welty's always remains: a favorite reminder of the great task to which I've set myself. My copy is well worn, heavily annotated: passages underlined, once, twice, in different-colored ink—one for each successive reading—or highlighted in yellow, dotted with stars or exclamation points in the margins that bear, on many pages, a record of my thoughts on a given day, my responses to Welty's words. That's one of the pleasures of beloved books: reading them again and again, going back to some seemingly familiar territory and finding things that went unnoticed before or that you might have seen in a different light. It's a way of encountering the self—of meeting a former self—the reader you were at another time.

I can't recall when I first read *One Writer's Beginnings*, nor exactly who I was back then. Two things come to mind: My mother was already lost to me—she had died when I was nineteen—and *that* great loss was pushing me toward some necessary articulation, toward becoming a writer. Perhaps my father, also a writer and professor, had suggested I read it to make sense of my own inclinations. Or perhaps I sought out *Beginnings* to make a connection with a writer from my native geography, from my Mississippi. I had long since encountered Welty's fiction, but meeting an author in autobiography is a different thing, a way to see behind the stories into the life that led to their making.

This is what strikes me on the very first page. Welty begins as we all do, rooted in a particular time and place, a child encountering the sensory world she inhabited at home in Jackson, Mississippi. She describes the sounds of that house: her parents signaling to each other from up and down the stairs, her father whistling, her mother humming the tune back to him; the clocks in the house chiming the hour in their different voices. All of it a dialogue, each call inviting an answer to which the child was acutely attuned. "Children, like animals," Welty writes, "use all their senses to discover the world." This is one of the humble gifts of her memoir, the generosity with which she shares her experience while reminding us of how similar we are despite how vastly different the particularities of our experience may be.

Reading the discoveries of her life offers not only revelation into the mind of a great writer but also an invitation to recall our own discoveries, to meet ourselves again in our memories. "It is our inward journey that leads us through time," she writes, "forward or back, seldom in a straight line, most often spiraling. Each of us is moving, changing, with respect to others. As we discover, we remember; remembering, we discover; and most intensely do we experience this when our separate journeys converge."

I did not have the opportunity to meet Miss Welty in person, and yet I feel a kind of intimacy meeting her in her words: a convergence of two women, two Mississippians—one white, one black—born more than half a century apart. It is that convergence, what Welty would call *confluence*, that each of us enacts when reading this slender and lovely narrative. Our separate journeys converging.

Even as the title proclaims its singularity, the origins of a particular writer, *One Writer's Beginnings* seems to me both timeless and necessary for any of us going about each day—a kind of primer for being a citizen of the world, for answering our own particular callings and joining the long conversation that is human history. Whether or not we are writers, we tell a story to ourselves about our lives, the arc of them—what gives meaning and purpose, and connects us to others.

I am reminded of that each time I read *One Writer's Beginnings*, each time I meet myself in her words, each time I am compelled to respond in the margins to some new discovery. An answering that expands the conversation. I think she'd welcome that.

Natasha Trethewey

When I was young enough to still spend a long time buttoning my shoes in the morning, I'd listen toward the hall: Daddy upstairs was shaving in the bathroom and Mother downstairs was frying the bacon. They would begin whistling back and forth to each other up and down the stairwell. My father would whistle his phrase, my mother would try to whistle, then hum hers back. It was their duet. I drew my buttonhook in and out and listened to it—I knew it was "The Merry Widow." The difference was, their song almost floated with laughter: how different from the record, which growled from the beginning, as if the Victrola were only slowly being wound up. They kept it running between them, up and down the stairs where I was now just about ready to run clattering down and show them my shoes.

I

Listening

In our house on North Congress Street in Jackson, Mississippi, where I was born, the oldest of three children, in 1909, we grew up to the striking of clocks. There was a mission-style oak grandfather clock standing in the hall, which sent its gong-like strokes through the livingroom, diningroom, kitchen, and pantry, and up the sounding board of the stairwell. Through the night, it could find its way into our ears; sometimes, even on the sleeping porch, midnight could wake us up. My parents' bedroom had a smaller striking clock that answered it. Though the kitchen clock did nothing but show the time, the diningroom clock was a cuckoo clock with weights on long chains, on one of which my baby brother, after climbing on a chair to the top of the china closet, once succeeded in suspending the cat for a moment. I don't know whether or not my father's Ohio family, in having been Swiss back in the 1700s before the first three Welty brothers came to America, had anything to do with this; but we all of us have been time-minded all our lives. This was good at least for a future fiction writer, being able to learn so penetratingly, and almost first of all, about chronology. It was one of a good many things I learned almost without knowing it; it would be there when I needed it.

My father loved all instruments that would instruct and fascinate. His place to keep things was the drawer in the "library table" where lying on top of his folded maps was a telescope with brass extensions, to find the moon and the Big Dipper after supper in our front yard, and to keep appointments with eclipses. There was a folding Kodak that was brought out for Christmas, birthdays, and trips. In the back of the drawer you could find a magnifying glass, a kaleidoscope, and a gyroscope kept in a black buckram box, which he would set dancing for us on a string pulled tight. He had also supplied himself with an assortment of puzzles composed of metal rings and intersecting links and keys chained together, impossible for the rest of us, however patiently shown, to take apart; he had an almost childlike love of the ingenious.

In time, a barometer was added to our diningroom wall; but we didn't really need it. My father had the country boy's accurate knowledge of the weather and its skies. He went out and stood on our front steps first thing in the morning and took a look at it and a sniff. He was a pretty good weather prophet.

"Well, I'm *not*," my mother would say with enormous self-satisfaction.

He told us children what to do if we were lost in a strange country. "Look for where the sky is brightest along the horizon," he said. "That reflects the nearest river. Strike out for a river and you will find habitation." Eventualities were much on his mind. In his care for us children he cautioned us to

4

take measures against such things as being struck by lightning. He drew us all away from the windows during the severe electrical storms that are common where we live. My mother stood apart, scoffing at caution as a character failing. "Why, I always loved a storm! High winds never bothered me in West Virginia! Just listen at that! I wasn't a bit afraid of a little lightning and thunder! I'd go out on the mountain and spread my arms wide and *run* in a good big storm!"

So I developed a strong meteorological sensibility. In years ahead when I wrote stories, atmosphere took its influential role from the start. Commotion in the weather and the inner feelings aroused by such a hovering disturbance emerged connected in dramatic form. (I tried a tornado first, in a story called "The Winds.")

From our earliest Christmas times, Santa Claus brought us toys that instruct boys and girls (separately) how to build things—stone blocks cut to the castle-building style, Tinker Toys, and Erector sets. Daddy made for us himself elaborate kites that needed to be taken miles out of town to a pasture long enough (and my father was not afraid of horses and cows watching) for him to run with and get up on a long cord to which my mother held the spindle, and then we children were given it to hold, tugging like something alive at our hands. They were beautiful, sound, shapely box kites, smelling delicately of office glue for their entire short lives. And of course, as soon as the boys attained anywhere near the right age, there was an electric train, the engine with its pea-sized working headlight, its line of cars, tracks equipped with switches, semaphores, its station, its bridges, and its tunnel, which blocked off all other traffic in the upstairs hall. Even from downstairs, and through the cries of excited children, the elegant rush and click of the train could be heard through the ceiling, running around and around its figure eight.

All of this, but especially the train, represents my father's fondest beliefs—in progress, in the future. With these gifts, he was preparing his children.

And so was my mother with her different gifts.

I learned from the age of two or three that any room in our house, at any time of day, was there to read in, or to be read to. My mother read to me. She'd read to me in the big bedroom in the mornings, when we were in her rocker together, which ticked in rhythm as we rocked, as though we had a cricket accompanying the story. She'd read to me in the diningroom on winter afternoons in front of the coal fire, with our cuckoo clock ending the story with "Cuckoo," and at night when I'd got in my own bed. I must have given her no peace. Sometimes she read to me in the kitchen while she sat churning, and the churning sobbed along with *any* story. It was my ambition to have her read to me while *I* churned; once she granted my wish, but she read off my story before I brought her butter. She was an expressive reader. When she was reading "Puss in Boots," for instance, it was impossible not to know that she distrusted *all* cats.

It had been startling and disappointing to me to find out

that story books had been written by *people,* that books were not natural wonders, coming up of themselves like grass. Yet regardless of where they came from, I cannot remember a time when I was not in love with them—with the books themselves, cover and binding and the paper they were printed on, with their smell and their weight and with their possession in my arms, captured and carried off to myself. Still illiterate, I was ready for them, committed to all the reading I could give them.

Neither of my parents had come from homes that could afford to buy many books, but though it must have been something of a strain on his salary, as the youngest officer in a young insurance company, my father was all the while carefully selecting and ordering away for what he and Mother thought we children should grow up with. They bought first for the future.

Besides the bookcase in the livingroom, which was always called "the library," there were the encyclopedia tables and dictionary stand under windows in our diningroom. Here to help us grow up arguing around the diningroom table were the Unabridged Webster, the Columbia Encyclopedia, Compton's Pictured Encyclopedia, the Lincoln Library of Information, and later the Book of Knowledge. And the year we moved into our new house, there was room to celebrate it with the new 1925 edition of the Britannica, which my father, his face always deliberately turned toward the future, was of course disposed to think better than any previous edition.

In "the library," inside the mission-style bookcase with its three diamond-latticed glass doors, with my father's Morris chair and the glass-shaded lamp on its table beside it, were books I could soon begin on—and I did, reading them all alike and as they came, straight down their rows, top shelf to bottom. There was the set of Stoddard's Lectures, in all its late nineteenth-century vocabulary and vignettes of peasant life and quaint beliefs and customs, with matching halftone illustrations: Vesuvius erupting, Venice by moonlight, gypsies glimpsed by their campfires. I didn't know then the clue they were to my father's longing to see the rest of the world. I read straight through his other love-from-afar: the Victrola Book of the Opera, with opera after opera in synopsis, with portraits in costume of Melba, Caruso, Galli-Curci, and Geraldine Farrar, some of whose voices we could listen to on our Red Seal records.

My mother read secondarily for information; she sank as a hedonist into novels. She read Dickens in the spirit in which she would have eloped with him. The novels of her girlhood that had stayed on in her imagination, besides those of Dickens and Scott and Robert Louis Stevenson, were *Jane Eyre, Trilby, The Woman in White, Green Mansions, King Solomon's Mines*. Marie Corelli's name would crop up but I understood she had gone out of favor with my mother, who had only kept *Ardath* out of loyalty. In time she absorbed herself in Galsworthy, Edith Wharton, above all in Thomas Mann of the *Joseph* volumes.

St. Elmo was not in our house; I saw it often in other houses. This wildly popular Southern novel is where all the Edna Earles in our population started coming from. They're all named for the heroine, who succeeded in bringing a dissolute, sinning roué and atheist of a lover (St. Elmo) to his knees. My mother was able to forgo it. But she remembered the classic advice given to rose growers on how to water their bushes long enough: "Take a chair and *St. Elmo*."

To both my parents I owe my early acquaintance with a beloved Mark Twain. There was a full set of Mark Twain and a short set of Ring Lardner in our bookcase, and those were the volumes that in time united us all, parents and children.

Reading everything that stood before me was how I came upon a worn old book without a back that had belonged to my father as a child. It was called *Sanford and Merton*. Is there anyone left who recognizes it, I wonder? It is the famous moral tale written by Thomas Day in the 1780s, but of him no mention is made on the title page of *this* book; here it is *Sanford and Merton in Words of One Syllable* by Mary Godolphin. Here are the rich boy and the poor boy and Mr. Barlow, their teacher and interlocutor, in long discourses alternating with dramatic scenes—danger and rescue allotted to the rich and the poor respectively. It may have only words of one syllable, but one of them is "quoth." It ends with not one but two morals, both engraved on rings: "Do what you ought, come what may," and "If we would be great, we must first learn to be good."

This book was lacking its front cover, the back held on by strips of pasted paper, now turned golden, in several layers, and the pages stained, flecked, and tattered around the edges; its garish illustrations had come unattached but were preserved, laid in. I had the feeling even in my heedless childhood that this was the only book my father as a little boy had had of his own. He had held onto it, and might have gone to sleep on its coverless face: he had lost his mother when he was seven. My father had never made any mention to his own children of the book, but he had brought it along with him from Ohio to our house and shelved it in our bookcase.

My mother had brought from West Virginia that set of Dickens; those books looked sad, too—they had been through fire and water before I was born, she told me, and there they were, lined up—as I later realized, waiting for *me*.

I was presented, from as early as I can remember, with books of my own, which appeared on my birthday and Christmas morning. Indeed, my parents could not give me books enough. They must have sacrificed to give me on my sixth or seventh birthday—it was after I became a reader for myself—the ten-volume set of Our Wonder World. These were beautifully made, heavy books I would lie down with on the floor in front of the diningroom hearth, and more often than the rest volume 5, *Every Child's Story Book*, was under my eyes. There were the fairy tales—Grimm, Andersen, the English, the French, "Ali Baba and the Forty Thieves"; and there was Aesop and Reynard the Fox; there were the myths and legends, Robin Hood, King Arthur, and St. George and the Dragon, even the history of Joan of Arc; a whack of *Pilgrim's Progress* and a long piece of *Gulliver*. They all carried their classic illustrations. I located myself in these pages and could go straight to the stories and pictures I loved; very often "The Yellow Dwarf" was first choice, with Walter Crane's Yellow Dwarf in full color making his terrifying appearance flanked by turkeys. Now that volume is as worn and backless and hanging apart as my father's poor *Sanford and Merton*. The precious page with Edward Lear's "Jumblies" on it has been in danger of slipping out for all these years. One measure of my love for Our Wonder World was that for a long time I wondered if I would go through fire and water for it as my mother had done for Charles Dickens; and the only comfort was to think I could ask my mother to do it for me.

I believe I'm the only child I know of who grew up with this treasure in the house. I used to ask others, "Did you have Our Wonder World?" I'd have to tell them The Book of Knowledge could not hold a candle to it.

I live in gratitude to my parents for initiating me—and as early as I begged for it, without keeping me waiting—into knowledge of the word, into reading and spelling, by way of the alphabet. They taught it to me at home in time for me to begin to read before starting to school. I believe the alphabet is no longer considered an essential piece of equipment for traveling through life. In my day it was the keystone to knowledge. You learned the alphabet as you learned to count to ten, as you learned "Now I lay me" and the Lord's Prayer and your father's and mother's name and address and telephone number, all in case you were lost.

My love for the alphabet, which endures, grew out of reciting it but, before that, out of seeing the letters on the page. In my own story books, before I could read them for myself, I fell in love with various winding, enchanted-looking initials drawn by Walter Crane at the heads of fairy tales. In "Once upon a time," an "O" had a rabbit running it as a treadmill, his feet upon flowers. When the day came, years later, for me to see the Book of Kells, all the wizardry of letter, initial, and word swept over me a thousand times over, and the illumination, the gold, seemed a part of the word's beauty and holiness that had been there from the start.

Learning stamps you with its moments. Childhood's learning is made up of moments. It isn't steady. It's a pulse.

In a children's art class, we sat in a ring on kindergarten chairs and drew three daffodils that had just been picked out of the yard; and while I was drawing, my sharpened yellow pencil and the cup of the yellow daffodil gave off whiffs just alike. That the pencil doing the drawing should give off the same smell as the flower it drew seemed part of the art lesson—as shouldn't it be? Children, like animals, use all their senses to discover the world. Then artists come along and discover it the same way, all over again. Here and there, it's the same world. Or now and then we'll hear from an artist who's never lost it.

In my sensory education I include my physical awareness of the *word*. Of a certain word, that is; the connection it has with what it stands for. At around age six, perhaps, I was standing by myself in our front yard waiting for supper, just at that hour in a late summer day when the sun is already below the horizon and the risen full moon in the visible sky stops being chalky and begins to take on light. There comes the moment, and I saw it then, when the moon goes from flat to round. For the first time it met my eyes as a globe. The word "moon" came into my mouth as though fed to me out of a silver spoon. Held in my mouth the moon became a word. It had the roundness of a Concord grape Grandpa took off his vine and gave me to suck out of its skin and swallow whole, in Ohio.

This love did not prevent me from living for years in foolish error about the moon. The new moon just appearing in the west was the rising moon to me. The new should be rising. And in early childhood the sun and moon, those opposite reigning powers, I just as easily assumed rose in east and west respectively in their opposite sides of the sky, and like partners in a reel they advanced, sun from the east, moon from the west, crossed over (when I wasn't looking) and went down on the other side. My father couldn't have known I believed that when, bending behind me and guiding my shoulder, he positioned me at our telescope in the front yard and, with careful adjustment of the focus, brought the moon close to me.

The night sky over my childhood Jackson was velvety black. I could see the full constellations in it and call their names; when I could read, I knew their myths. Though I was always waked for eclipses, and indeed carried to the window as an infant in arms and shown Halley's Comet in my sleep, and though I'd been taught at our diningroom table about the solar system and knew the earth revolved around the sun, and our moon around us, I never found out the moon didn't come up in the west until I was a writer and Herschel Brickell, the literary critic, told me after I misplaced it in a story. He said valuable words to me about my new profession: "Always be sure you get your moon in the right part of the sky."

My mother always sang to her children. Her voice came out just a little bit in the minor key. "Wee Willie Winkie's" song was wonderfully sad when she sang the lullabies.

"Oh, but now there's a record. She could have her own record to listen to," my father would have said. For there came a Victrola record of "Bobby Shafftoe" and "Rock-a-Bye Baby," all of Mother's lullabies, which could be played to take her place. Soon I was able to play her my own lullabies all day long.

Our Victrola stood in the diningroom. I was allowed to climb onto the seat of a diningroom chair to wind it, start the record turning, and set the needle playing. In a second

I'd jumped to the floor, to spin or march around the table as the music called for—now there were all the other records I could play too. I skinned back onto the chair just in time to lift the needle at the end, stop the record and turn it over, then change the needle. That brass receptacle with a hole in the lid gave off a metallic smell like human sweat, from all the hot needles that were fed it. Winding up, dancing, being cocked to start and stop the record, was of course all in one the act of *listening*—to "Overture to *Daughter of the Regiment*," "Selections from *The Fortune Teller*," "Kiss Me Again," "Gypsy Dance from *Carmen*," "Stars and Stripes Forever," "When the Midnight Choo-Choo Leaves for Alabam," or whatever came next. Movement must be at the very heart of listening.

Ever since I was first read to, then started reading to myself, there has never been a line read that I didn't *hear*. As my eyes followed the sentence, a voice was saying it silently to me. It isn't my mother's voice, or the voice of any person I can identify, certainly not my own. It is human, but inward, and it is inwardly that I listen to it. It is to me the voice of the story or the poem itself. The cadence, whatever it is that asks you to believe, the feeling that resides in the printed word, reaches me through the reader-voice. I have supposed, but never found out, that this is the case with all readers— to read as listeners—and with all writers, to write as listeners. It may be part of the desire to write. The sound of what falls on the page begins the process of testing it for truth, for me. Whether I am right to trust so far I don't know. By now

I don't know whether I could do either one, reading or writing, without the other.

My own words, when I am at work on a story, I hear too as they go, in the same voice that I hear when I read in books. When I write and the sound of it comes back to my ears, then I act to make my changes. I have always trusted this voice.

In that vanished time in small-town Jackson, most of the ladies I was familiar with, the mothers of my friends in the neighborhood, were busiest when they were sociable. In the afternoons there was regular visiting up and down the little grid of residential streets. Everybody had calling cards, even certain children; and newborn babies themselves were properly announced by sending out their tiny engraved calling cards attached with a pink or blue bow to those of their parents. Graduation presents to high-school pupils were often "card cases." On the hall table in every house the first thing you saw was a silver tray waiting to receive more calling cards on top of the stack already piled up like jackstraws; they were never thrown away.

My mother let none of this idling, as she saw it, pertain to her; she went her own way with or without her calling cards, and though she was fond of her friends and they were fond of her, she had little time for small talk. At first, I hadn't known what I'd missed.

When we at length bought our first automobile, one of

our neighbors was often invited to go with us on the family Sunday afternoon ride. In Jackson it was counted an affront to the neighbors to start out for anywhere with an empty seat in the car. My mother sat in the back with her friend, and I'm told that as a small child I would ask to sit in the middle, and say as we started off, "Now *talk*."

There was dialogue throughout the lady's accounts to my mother. "I said" ... "He said" ... "And I'm told she very plainly said" ... "It was midnight before they finally heard, and what do you think it *was*?"

What I loved about her stories was that everything happened in *scenes*. I might not catch on to what the root of the trouble was in all that happened, but my ear told me it was dramatic. Often she said, "The crisis had come!"

This same lady was one of Mother's callers on the telephone who always talked a long time. I knew who it was when my mother would only reply, now and then, "Well, I declare," or "You don't say so," or "Surely not." She'd be standing at the wall telephone, listening against her will, and I'd sit on the stairs close by her. Our telephone had a little bar set into the handle which had to be pressed and held down to keep the connection open, and when her friend had said goodbye, my mother needed me to prize her fingers loose from the little bar; her grip had become paralyzed. "What did she say?" I asked.

"She wasn't *saying* a thing in this world," sighed my mother. "She was just ready to talk, that's all."

My mother was right. Years later, beginning with my story "Why I Live at the P.O.," I wrote reasonably often in the form of a monologue that takes possession of the speaker. How much more gets told besides!

This lady told everything in her sweet, marveling voice, and meant every word of it kindly. She enjoyed my company perhaps even more than my mother's. She invited me to catch her doodlebugs; under the trees in her backyard were dozens of their holes. When you stuck a broom straw down one and called, "Doodlebug, doodlebug, your house is on fire and all your children are burning up," she believed this is why the doodlebug came running out of the hole. This was why I loved to call up her doodlebugs instead of ours.

My mother could never have told me her stories, and I think I knew why even then: my mother didn't believe them. But I could listen to this murmuring lady all day. She believed everything she heard, like the doodlebug. And so did I.

This was a day when ladies' and children's clothes were very often made at home. My mother cut out all the dresses and her little boys' rompers, and a sewing woman would come and spend the day upstairs in the sewing room fitting and stitching them all. This was Fannie. This old black sewing woman, along with her speed and dexterity, brought along a great provision of up-to-the-minute news. She spent her life going from family to family in town and worked right in its bosom, and nothing could stop her. My mother would try, while I stood being pinned up. "Fannie, I'd rather Eudora didn't hear that." "That" would be just what I was longing to hear, whatever it was. "I don't want her exposed to gossip"—as if gossip were measles and I could catch it. I did catch some of it but not enough. "Mrs. O'Neil's oldest daughter she had her wedding dress *tried on,* and all her fine underclothes featherstitched and ribbon run in and then—" "I think that will do, Fannie," said my mother. It was tantalizing never to be exposed long enough to hear the end.

Fannie was the worldliest old woman to be imagined. She could do whatever her hands were doing without having to stop talking; and she could speak in a wonderfully derogatory way with any number of pins stuck in her mouth. Her hands steadied me like claws as she stumped on her knees around me, tacking me together. The gist of her tale would be lost on me, but Fannie didn't bother about the ear she was telling it to; she just liked telling. She was like an author. In fact, for a good deal of what she said, I daresay she *was* the author.

Long before I wrote stories, I listened for stories. Listening *for* them is something more acute than listening *to* them. I suppose it's an early form of participation in what goes on. Listening children know stories are *there.* When their elders sit and begin, children are just waiting and hoping for one to come out, like a mouse from its hole.

It was taken entirely for granted that there wasn't any

lying in our family, and I was advanced in adolescence before I realized that in plenty of homes where I played with schoolmates and went to their parties, children lied to their parents and parents lied to their children and to each other. It took me a long time to realize that these very same everyday lies, and the stratagems and jokes and tricks and dares that went with them, were in fact the basis of the *scenes* I so well loved to hear about and hoped for and treasured in the conversation of adults.

My instinct—the dramatic instinct—was to lead me, eventually, on the right track for a storyteller: the *scene* was full of hints, pointers, suggestions, and promises of things to find out and know about human beings. I had to grow up and learn to listen for the unspoken as well as the spoken— and to know a truth, I also had to recognize a lie.

It was when my mother came out onto the sleeping porch to tell me goodnight that her trial came. The sudden silence in the double bed meant my younger brothers had both keeled over in sleep, and I in the single bed at my end of the porch would be lying electrified, waiting for this to be the night when she'd tell me what she'd promised for so long. Just as she bent to kiss me I grabbed her and asked: "Where do babies come from?"

My poor mother! But something saved her every time. Almost any night I put the baby question to her, suddenly, as if the whole outdoors exploded, Professor Holt would start

20

to sing. The Holts lived next door; he taught penmanship (the Palmer Method), typing, bookkeeping, and shorthand at the high school. His excitable voice traveled out of their diningroom windows across the two driveways between our houses, and up to our upstairs sleeping porch. His wife, usually so quiet and gentle, was his uncannily spirited accompanist at the piano. "High-ho! Come to the Fair!" he'd sing, unless he sang "Oho ye oho ye, who's bound for the ferry, the briar's in bud and the sun's going down!"

"Dear, this isn't a very good time for you to hear Mother, is it?"

She couldn't get started. As soon as she'd whisper something, Professor Holt galloped into the chorus, "And 'tis but a penny to Twickenham town!" "Isn't that enough?" she'd ask me. She'd told me that the mother and the father had to both *want* the baby. This couldn't be enough. I knew she was not trying to fib to me, for she never did fib, but also I could not help but know she was not really *telling* me. And more than that, I was afraid of what I was going to hear next. This was partly because she wanted to tell me in the dark. I thought *she* might be afraid. In something like childish hopelessness I thought she probably *couldn't* tell, just as she *couldn't* lie.

On the night we came the closest to having it over with, she started to tell me without being asked, and I ruined it by yelling, "Mother, look at the lightning bugs!"

In those days, the dark was dark. And all the dark out

21

there was filled with the soft, near lights of lightning bugs. They were everywhere, flashing on the slow, horizontal move, on the upswings, rising and subsiding in the soundless dark. Lightning bugs signaled and answered back without a stop, from down below all the way to the top of our sycamore tree. My mother just gave me a businesslike kiss and went on back to Daddy in their room at the front of the house. Distracted by lightning bugs, I had missed my chance. The fact is she never did tell me.

I doubt that any child I knew ever was told by her mother any more than I was about babies. In fact, I doubt that her own mother ever told her any more than she told me, though there were five brothers who were born after Mother, one after the other, and she was taking care of babies all her childhood.

Not being able to bring herself to open that door to reveal its secret, one of those days, she opened another door.

In my mother's bottom bureau drawer in her bedroom she kept treasures of hers in boxes, and had given me permission to play with one of them—a switch of her own chestnut-colored hair, kept in a heavy bright braid that coiled around like a snake inside a cardboard box. I hung it from her doorknob and unplaited it; it fell in ripples nearly to the floor, and it satisfied the Rapunzel in me to comb it out. But one day I noticed in the same drawer a small white cardboard box such as her engraved calling cards came in from the printing house. It was tightly closed, but I opened it, to find to my puzzlement and covetousness two polished buffalo nickels, embedded in white cotton. I rushed with this opened box to my mother and asked if I could run out and spend the nickels.

"No!" she exclaimed in a most passionate way. She seized the box into her own hands. I begged her; somehow I had started to cry. Then she sat down, drew me to her, and told me that I had had a little brother who had come before I did, and who had died as a baby before I was born. And these two nickels that I'd wanted to claim as my find were his. They had lain on his eyelids, for a purpose untold and unimaginable. "He was a fine little baby, my first baby, and he shouldn't have died. But he did. It was because your mother almost died at the same time," she told me. "In looking after me, they too nearly forgot about the little baby."

She'd told me the wrong secret—not how babies could come but how they could die, how they could be forgotten about.

I wondered in after years: how could my mother have kept those two coins? Yet how could someone like herself have disposed of them in any way at all? She suffered from a morbid streak which in all the life of the family reached out on occasions—the worst occasions—and touched us, clung around us, making it worse for her; her unbearable moments could find nowhere to go.

The future story writer in the child I was must have taken unconscious note and stored it away then: one secret is liable to be revealed in the place of another that is harder to tell, and the substitute secret when nakedly exposed is often the more appalling.

Perhaps telling me what she did was made easier for my mother by the two secrets, told and still not told, being connected in her deepest feeling, more intimately than anyone ever knew, perhaps even herself. So far as I remember now, this is the only time this baby was ever mentioned in my presence. So far as I can remember, and I've tried, he was never mentioned in the presence of my father, for whom he had been named. I am only certain that my father, who could never bear pain very well, would not have been able to bear it.

It was my father (my mother told me at some later date) who saved her own life, after that baby was born. She had in fact been given up by the doctor, as she had long been unable to take any nourishment. (That was the illness when they'd cut her hair, which formed the switch in the same bureau drawer.) What had struck her was septicemia, in those days nearly always fatal. What my father did was to try champagne.

I once wondered where he, who'd come not very long before from an Ohio farm, had ever heard of such a remedy, such a measure. Or perhaps as far as he was concerned he invented it, out of the strength of desperation. It would have been desperation augmented because champagne couldn't be bought in Jackson. But somehow he knew what to do about that too. He telephoned to Canton, forty miles north, to an Italian orchard grower, Mr. Trolio, told him the necessity, and asked, begged, that he put a bottle of his wine on Number 3, which was due in a few minutes to stop in Canton to "take on water" (my father knew everything about train schedules). My father would be waiting to meet the train in Jackson. Mr. Trolio did—he sent the bottle in a bucket of ice and my father snatched it off the baggage car. He offered my mother a glass of chilled champagne and she drank it and kept it down. She was to live, after all.

Now, her hair was long again, it would reach in a braid down her back, and now I was her child. She hadn't died. And when I came, I hadn't died either. Would she ever? Would I ever? I couldn't face *ever*. I must have rushed into her lap, demanding her like a baby. And she had to put her first-born aside again, for me.

Of course it's easy to see why they both overprotected me, why my father, before I could wear a new pair of shoes for the first time, made me wait while he took out his thin silver pocket knife and with the point of the blade scored the polished soles all over, carefully, in a diamond pattern, to prevent me from sliding on the polished floor when I ran.

As I was to learn over and over again, my mother's mind was a mass of associations. Whatever happened would be forever paired for her with something that had happened before it, to one of us or to her. It became a private anniversary. Every time any possible harm came near me, she thought of how she lost her first child. When a Roman candle at Christmas backfired up my sleeve, she rushed to smother the blaze with the first thing she could grab, which was a dish towel hanging in the kitchen, and the burn on my arm became infected. I was nothing but proud of my sling, for I could wear it to school, and her repeated blaming of herself—for even my sling—puzzled and troubled me.

When my mother would tell me that she wanted me to have something because she as a child had never had it, I wanted, or I partly wanted, to give it back. All my life I continued to feel that bliss for me would have to imply my mother's deprivation or sacrifice. I don't think it would have occurred to her what a double emotion I felt, and indeed I know that it was being unfair to her, for what she said was simply the truth.

"I'm going to let you go to the Century Theatre with your father tonight on my ticket. I'd rather you saw *Blossom Time* than go myself."

In the Century first-row balcony, where their seats always were, I'd be sitting beside my father at this hour beyond my bedtime carried totally away by the performance, and then suddenly the thought of my mother staying home with my sleeping younger brothers, missing the spectacle at this moment before my eyes, and doing without all the excitement and wonder that filled my being, would arrest me and I could hardly bear my pleasure for my guilt.

There is no wonder that a passion for independence sprang up in me at the earliest age. It took me a long time to manage the independence, for I loved those who protected me—and I wanted inevitably to protect them back. I have never managed to handle the guilt. In the act and the course of writing stories, these are two of the springs, one bright, one dark, that feed the stream.

When I was six or seven, I was taken out of school and put to bed for several months for an ailment the doctor described as "fast-beating heart." I felt all right—perhaps I felt too good. It was the feeling of suspense. At any rate, I was allowed to occupy all day my parents' double bed in the front upstairs bedroom.

I was supposed to rest, and the little children didn't get to run in and excite me often. Davis School was as close as across the street. I could keep up with it from the window beside me, hear the principal ring her bell, see which children were tardy, watch my classmates eat together at recess: I knew their sandwiches. I was homesick for school; my mother made time for teaching me arithmetic and hearing my spelling.

An opulence of story books covered my bed; it was the "Land of Counterpane." As I read away, I was Rapunzel, or the Goose Girl, or the Princess Labam in one of the *Thousand and One Nights* who mounted the roof of her palace every night and of her own radiance faithfully lighted the

27

whole city just by reposing there, and I daydreamed I could light Davis School from across the street.

But I never dreamed I could learn as long as I was away from the schoolroom, and that bits of enlightenment far-reaching in my life went on as ever in their own good time. After they'd told me goodnight and tucked me in—although I knew that after I'd finally fallen asleep they'd pick me up and carry me away—my parents draped the lampshade with a sheet of the daily paper, which was tilted, like a hatbrim, so that they could sit in their rockers in a lighted part of the room and I could supposedly go to sleep in the protected dark of the bed. They sat talking. What was thus dramatically made a present of to me was the secure sense of the hidden observer. As long as I could make myself keep awake, I was free to listen to every word my parents said between them.

I don't remember that any secrets were revealed to me, nor do I remember any avid curiosity on my part to learn something I wasn't supposed to—perhaps I was too young to know what to listen for. But I was present in the room with the chief secret there was—the two of them, father and mother, sitting there as one. I was conscious of this secret and of my fast-beating heart in step together, as I lay in the slant-shaded light of the room, with a brown, pear-shaped scorch in the newspaper shade where it had become overheated once.

What they talked about I have no idea, and the subject

was not what mattered to me. It was no doubt whatever a young married couple spending their first time privately in each other's company in the long, probably harried day would talk about. It was the murmur of their voices, the back-and-forth, the unnoticed stretching away of time between my bedtime and theirs, that made me bask there at my distance. What I felt was not that I was excluded from them but that I was included, in—and because of—what I could hear of their voices and what I could see of their faces in the cone of yellow light under the brown-scorched shade.

I suppose I was exercising as early as then the turn of mind, the nature of temperament, of a privileged observer; and owing to the way I became so, it turned out that I became the loving kind.

A conscious act grew out of this by the time I began to write stories: getting my distance, a prerequisite of my understanding of human events, is the way I begin work. Just as, of course, it was an initial step when, in my first journalism job, I stumbled into making pictures with a camera. Frame, proportion, perspective, the values of light and shade, all are determined by the distance of the observing eye.

I have always been shy physically. This in part tended to keep me from rushing into things, including relationships, headlong. Not rushing headlong, though I may have wanted to, but beginning to write stories about people, I drew near slowly; noting and guessing, apprehending, hoping, drawing my eventual conclusions out of my own heart, I *did* venture closer to where I wanted to go. As time and my imagination led me on, I did plunge.

From the first I was clamorous to learn—I wanted to know and begged to be told not so much what, or how, or why, or where, as when. How soon?

> *Pear tree by the garden gate,*
> *How much longer must I wait?*

This rhyme from one of my nursery books was the one that spoke for me. But I lived not at all unhappily in this craving, for my wild curiosity was in large part suspense, which carries its own secret pleasure. And so one of the godmothers of fiction was already bending over me.

When I was five years old, I knew the alphabet, I'd been vaccinated (for smallpox), and I could read. So my mother walked across the street to Jefferson Davis Grammar School and asked the principal if she would allow me to enter the first grade after Christmas.

"Oh, all right," said Miss Duling. "Probably the best thing you could do with her."

Miss Duling, a lifelong subscriber to perfection, was a figure of authority, the most whole-souled I have ever come to know. She was a dedicated schoolteacher who denied herself all she might have done or whatever other way she might have lived (this possibility was the last that could have occurred to us, her subjects in school). I believe she came of well-off people, well-educated, in Kentucky, and certainly old photographs show she was a beautiful, high-spirited-looking young lady—and came down to Jackson to its new grammar school that was going begging for a principal. She must have earned next to nothing; Mississippi then as now was the nation's lowest-ranking state economically, and our legislature has always shown a painfully loud reluctance to give money to public education. That challenge *brought* her.

In the long run she came into touch, as teacher or principal, with three generations of Jacksonians. My parents had not, but everybody else's parents had gone to school to her. She'd taught most of our leaders somewhere along the line. When she wanted something done—some civic oversight corrected, some injustice made right overnight, or even a tree spared that the fool telephone people were about to cut down—she telephoned the mayor, or the chief of police, or the president of the power company, or the head doctor at the hospital, or the judge in charge of a case, or whoever, and calling them by their first names, *told* them. It is impossible to imagine her meeting with anything less than compliance. The ringing of her brass bell from their days at Davis School would still be in their ears. She also proposed a spelling match between the fourth grade at Davis School and the Mississippi Legislature, who went through with it; and that told the Legislature.

Her standards were very high and of course inflexible, her

authority was total; why *wouldn't* this carry with it a brass bell that could be heard ringing for a block in all directions? That bell belonged to the figure of Miss Duling as though it grew directly out of her right arm, as wings grew out of an angel or a tail out of the devil. When we entered, marching, into her school, by strictest teaching, surveillance, and order we learned grammar, arithmetic, spelling, reading, writing, and geography; and she, not the teachers, I believe, wrote out the examinations: need I tell you, they were "hard."

She's not the only teacher who has influenced me, but Miss Duling, in some fictional shape or form, has stridden into a larger part of my work than I'd realized until now. She emerges in my perhaps inordinate number of school-teacher characters. I loved those characters in the writing. But I did not, in life, love Miss Duling. I was afraid of her high-arched bony nose, her eyebrows lifted in half-circles above her hooded, brilliant eyes, and of the Kentucky R's in her speech, and the long steps she took in her hightop shoes. I did nothing but fear her bearing-down authority, and did not connect this (as of course we were meant to) with our own need or desire to learn, perhaps because I already had this wish, and did not need to be driven.

She was impervious to lies or foolish excuses or the insufferable plea of not knowing any better. She wasn't going to have any frills, either, at Davis School. When a new governor moved into the mansion, he sent his daughter to Davis School; her name was Lady Rachel Conner. Miss Duling at once called the governor to the telephone and told him, "She'll be plain Rachel here."

Miss Duling dressed as plainly as a Pilgrim on a Thanksgiving poster we made in the schoolroom, in a longish black-and-white checked gingham dress, a bright thick wool sweater the red of a railroad lantern—she'd knitted it herself—black stockings and her narrow elegant feet in black hightop shoes with heels you could hear coming, rhythmical as a parade drum down the hall. Her silky black curly hair was drawn back out of curl, fastened by high combs, and knotted behind. She carried her spectacles on a gold chain hung around her neck. Her gaze was in general sweeping, then suddenly at the point of concentration upon you. With a swing of her bell that took her whole right arm and shoulder, she rang it, militant and impartial, from the head of the front steps of Davis School when it was time for us all to line up, girls on one side, boys on the other. We were to march past her into the school building, while the fourth-grader she nabbed played time on the piano, mostly to a tune we could have skipped to, but we didn't skip into Davis School.

Little recess (open-air exercises) and big recess (lunchboxes from home opened and eaten on the grass, on the girls' side and the boys' side of the yard) and dismissal were also regulated by Miss Duling's bell. The bell was also used to catch us off guard with fire drill.

It was examinations that drove my wits away, as all emergencies do. Being expected to measure up was paralysing. I failed to make 100 on my spelling exam because I missed one word and that word was "uncle." Mother, as I knew she would, took it personally. "You couldn't spell *uncle*? When you've got those five perfectly splendid uncles in West Virginia? What would *they* say to that?"

It was never that Mother wanted me to beat my classmates in grades; what she wanted was for me to have my answers right. It was unclouded perfection I was up against.

My father was much more tolerant of possible error. He only said, as he steeply and impeccably sharpened my pencils on examination morning, "Now just keep remembering: the examinations were made out for the *average* student to pass. That's the majority. And if the majority can pass, think how much better *you* can do."

I looked to my mother, who had her own opinions about the majority. My father wished to treat it with respect, she didn't. I'd been born left-handed, but the habit was broken when I entered the first grade in Davis School. My father had insisted. He pointed out that everything in life had been made for the convenience of right-handed people, because they were the majority, and he often used "what the majority wants" as a criterion for what was for the best. My mother said she could not promise him, could not promise him at all, that I wouldn't stutter as a consequence. Mother had been born left-handed too; her family consisted of five left-handed brothers, a left-handed mother, and a father who could write with both hands at the same time, also backwards and forwards and upside down, different words with each hand. She had been broken of it when she was young, and she said she used to stutter.

"But you still stutter," I'd remind her, only to hear her say loftily, "You should have heard me when I was your age."

In my childhood days, a great deal of stock was put, in general, in the value of doing well in school. Both daily newspapers in Jackson saw the honor roll as news and published the lists, and the grades, of all the honor students. The city fathers gave the children who made the honor roll free season tickets to the baseball games down at the grandstand. We all attended and all worshiped some player on the Jackson Senators: I offered up my 100's in arithmetic and spelling, reading and writing, attendance and, yes, deportment—I must have been a prig!—to Red McDermott, the third baseman. And our happiness matched that of knowing Miss Duling was on her summer vacation, far, far away in Kentucky.

Every school week, visiting teachers came on their days for special lessons. On Mondays, the singing teacher blew into the room fresh from the early outdoors, singing in her high soprano "How do you do?" to do-mi-sol-do, and we responded in chorus from our desks, "I'm ve-ry well" to do-sol-mi-do. Miss Johnson taught us rounds—"Row row row your boat gently down the stream"—and "Little Sir Echo," with half the room singing the words and the other half being the echo, a competition. She was from the North, and she was the one who wanted us all to stop the Christmas carols and see snow. The snow falling that morning outside the window was the first most of us had ever seen, and Miss Johnson threw up the window and held out wide her own black cape and caught flakes on it and ran, as fast as she could go, up and down the aisles to show us the real thing before it melted.

Thursday was Miss Eyrich and Miss Eyrich was Thursday. She came to give us physical training. She wasted no time on nonsense. Without greeting, we were marched straight outside and summarily divided into teams (no choosing sides), put on the mark, and ordered to get set for a relay race. Miss Eyrich cracked out "Go!" Dread rose in my throat. My head swam. Here was my turn, nearly upon me. (Wait, have I been touched—was that slap the touch? Go on! Do I go on without our passing a word? What word? Now am I racing too fast to turn around? Now I'm nearly home, but where is the hand waiting for mine to touch? Am I too late? Have I lost the whole race for our side?) I lost the relay race for our side before I started, through living ahead of myself, dreading to make my start, feeling too late prematurely, and standing transfixed by emergency, trying to think of a password. Thursdays still can make me hear Miss Eyrich's voice. "On your mark—get set—GO!"

Very composedly and very slowly, the art teacher, who visited each room on Fridays, paced the aisle and looked down over your shoulder at what you were drawing for her.

This was Miss Ascher. Coming from behind you, her deep, resonant voice reached you without being a word at all, but a sort of purr. It was much the sound given out by our family doctor when he read the thermometer and found you were running a slight fever: "Um-hm. Um-hm." Both alike, they let you go right ahead with it.

The school toilets were in the boys' and girls' respective basements. After Miss Duling had rung to dismiss school, a friend and I were making our plans for Saturday from adjoining cubicles. "Can you come spend the day with me?" I called out, and she called back, "I might could."

"Who—said—MIGHT—COULD?" It sounded like "Fe Fi Fo Fum!"

We both were petrified, for we knew whose deep measured words those were that came from just outside our doors. That was the voice of Mrs. McWillie, who taught the other fourth grade across the hall from ours. She was not even our teacher, but a very heavy, stern lady who dressed entirely in widow's weeds with a pleated black shirtwaist with a high net collar and velvet ribbon, and a black skirt to her ankles, with black circles under her eyes and a mournful, Presbyterian expression. We children took her to be a hundred years old. We held still.

"You might as well tell me," continued Mrs. McWillie. "I'm going to plant myself right here and wait till you come out. Then I'll see who it was I heard saying 'MIGHT-COULD.' "

If Elizabeth wouldn't go out, of course I wouldn't either. We knew her to be a teacher who would not flinch from standing there in the basement all afternoon, perhaps even all day Saturday. So we surrendered and came out. I priggishly hoped Elizabeth would clear it up which child it was—it wasn't me.

"So it's you." She regarded us as a brace, made no distinction: whoever didn't say it was guilty by association. "If I ever catch you down here one more time saying 'MIGHT-COULD,' I'm going to carry it to Miss Duling. You'll be kept in every day for a week! I hope you're both sufficiently ashamed of yourselves?" Saying "might-could" was bad, but saying it in the basement made bad grammar a sin. I knew Presbyterians believed that you could go to Hell.

Mrs. McWillie never scared us into grammar, of course. It was my first-year Latin teacher in high school who made me discover I'd fallen in love with it. It took Latin to thrust me into bona fide alliance with words in their true meaning. Learning Latin (once I was free of Caesar) fed my love for words upon words, words in continuation and modification, and the beautiful, sober, accretion of a sentence. I could see the achieved sentence finally standing there, as real, intact, and built to stay as the Mississippi State Capitol at the top of my street, where I could walk through it on my way to school and hear underfoot the echo of its marble floor, and over me the bell of its rotunda.

On winter's rainy days, the schoolrooms would grow

38

so dark that sometimes you couldn't see the figures on the blackboard. At that point, Mrs. McWillie, that stern fourth-grade teacher, would let her children close their books, and she would move, broad in widow's weeds like darkness itself, to the window and by what light there was she would stand and read aloud "The King of the Golden River." But I was excluded—in the other fourth grade, across the hall. Miss Louella Varnado, my teacher, didn't copy Mrs. McWillie; we had a spelling match: you could spell in the dark. I did not then suspect that there was any other way I could learn the story of "The King of the Golden River" than to have been assigned in the beginning to Mrs. McWillie's cowering fourth grade, then wait for her to treat you to it on the rainy day of her choice. I only now realize how much the treat depended, too, on there not having been money enough to put electric lights in Davis School. John Ruskin had to come in through courtesy of darkness. When in time I found the story in a book and read it to myself, it didn't seem to live up to my longings for a story with that name; as indeed, how could it?

Jackson's Carnegie Library was on the same street where our house was, on the other side of the State Capitol. "Through the Capitol" was the way to go to the Library. You could glide through it on your bicycle or even coast through on roller skates, though without family permission.

I never knew anyone who'd grown up in Jackson without being afraid of Mrs. Calloway, our librarian. She ran the

Library absolutely by herself, from the desk where she sat with her back to the books and facing the stairs, her dragon eye on the front door, where who knew what kind of person might come in from the public? SILENCE in big black letters was on signs tacked up everywhere. She herself spoke in her normally commanding voice; every word could be heard all over the Library above a steady seething sound coming from her electric fan; it was the only fan in the Library and stood on her desk, turned directly onto her streaming face.

As you came in from the bright outside, if you were a girl, she sent her strong eyes down the stairway to test you; if she could see through your skirt she sent you straight back home: you could just put on another petticoat if you wanted a book that badly from the public library. I was willing; I would do anything to read.

My mother was not afraid of Mrs. Calloway. She wished me to have my own library card to check out books for myself. She took me in to introduce me and I saw I had met a witch. "Eudora is nine years old and has my permission to read any book she wants from the shelves, children or adult," Mother said. "With the exception of *Elsie Dinsmore*," she added. Later she explained to me that she'd made this rule because Elsie the heroine, being made by her father to practice too long and hard at the piano, fainted and fell off the piano stool. "You're too impressionable, dear," she told me. "You'd read that and the very first thing you'd do, you'd fall off the piano stool." "Impressionable" was a new word.

I never hear it yet without the image that comes with it of falling straight off the piano stool.

Mrs. Calloway made her own rules about books. You could not take back a book to the Library on the same day you'd taken it out; it made no difference to her that you'd read every word in it and needed another to start. You could take out two books at a time and two only; this applied as long as you were a child and also for the rest of your life, to my mother as severely as to me. So two by two, I read library books as fast as I could go, rushing them home in the basket of my bicycle. From the minute I reached our house, I started to read. Every book I seized on, from *Bunny Brown and His Sister Sue at Camp Rest-a-While* to *Twenty Thousand Leagues under the Sea*, stood for the devouring wish to read being instantly granted. I knew this was bliss, knew it at the time. Taste isn't nearly so important; it comes in its own time. I wanted to read *immediately*. The only fear was that of books coming to an end.

My mother was very sharing of this feeling of insatiability. Now, I think of her as reading so much of the time while doing something else. In my mind's eye *The Origin of Species* is lying on the shelf in the pantry under a light dusting of flour—my mother was a bread maker; she'd pick it up, sit by the kitchen window and find her place, with one eye on the oven. I remember her picking up *The Man in Lower Ten* while my hair got dry enough to unroll from a load of kid curlers trying to make me like my idol, Mary Pickford.

A generation later, when my brother Walter was away in the Navy and his two little girls often spent the day in our house, I remember Mother reading the new issue of *Time* magazine while taking the part of the Wolf in a game of "Little Red Riding Hood" with the children. She'd just look up at the right time, long enough to answer—in character—"The better to eat you with, my dear," and go back to her place in the war news.

Both our parents had grown up in religious households. In our own family, we children were christened as babies, and were taught our prayers to say at night, and sent as we were growing up to Sunday school, but ours was never a church-going family. At home we did not, like Grandpa Welty, say grace at table. In this way we were variously different from most of the families we knew. On Sundays, Presbyterians were not allowed to eat hot food or read the funnypapers or travel the shortest journey; parents believed in Hell and believed tiny babies could go there. Baptists were not supposed to know, up until their dying day, how to play cards or dance. And so on. We went to the Methodist Episcopal Church South Sunday School, and of course we never saw anything strange about Methodists.

But we grew up in a religious-minded society. Even in high school, pupils were used to answering the history teacher's roll call with a perfectly recited verse from the Bible. (No fair "Jesus wept.")

In the primary department of Sunday school, we little girls rose up in taffeta dresses and hot white gloves, with a nickel for collection embedded inside our palms, and while elastic bands from our Madge Evans hats sawed us under the chin, we sang songs led and exhorted by Miss Hattie. This little lady was a wonder of animation, also dressed up, and she stood next to the piano making wild chopping motions with both arms together, a chairleg off one of our Sunday school chairs in her hand to beat time with, and no matter how loudly we sang, we could always hear her even louder: "Bring them in! Bring them in! Bring them in from the fields of sin! Bring the little ones to Jesus!" Those favorite Methodist hymns all sounded happy and pleased with the world, even though the words ran quite the other way. "Throw out the lifeline! Throw out the lifeline! Someone is sinking today!" went to a cheering tune. "I was sinking deep in sin, Far from the peaceful shore, Very deeply stained within, Sinking to rise no more" made you want to dance, and the chorus—"Love lifted me! Love lifted me! When nothing else would help, Love lifted me!"—would send you leaping. Those hymns set your feet moving like the march played on the piano for us to enter Davis School— "Dorothy, an Old English Dance" was the name of that, and of course so many of the Protestant hymns reached down to us from the same place; they *were* old English rounds and dance tunes, and Charles Wesley and the rest had—no wonder—taken them over.

• • •

Evangelists visited Jackson then; along with the Redpath Chautauqua and political speakings, they seemed to be part of August. Gypsy Smith was a great local favorite. He was an evangelist, but the term meant nothing like what it stands for today. He had no "team," no organization, no big business, no public address system; he wasn't a showman. Billy Sunday, a little later on, who preached with the athletics of a baseball player, threw off his coat when he got going, and in his shirtsleeves and red suspenders, he wound up and pitched his punchlines into the audience.

Gypsy Smith was a real Gypsy; in this may have lain part of his magnetism, though he spoke with sincerity too. He was so persuasive that, as night after night went by, he saved "everybody in Jackson," saved all the well-known businessmen on Capitol Street. They might well have been churchgoers already, but they never had been saved by Gypsy Smith. While amalgamated Jackson church choirs sang "Softly and Tenderly Jesus Is Calling" and "Just as I Am," Gypsy Smith called, and being saved—standing up and coming forward—swept Jackson like an epidemic. Most spectacular of all, the firebrand editor of the evening newspaper rose up and came forward one night. It made him lastingly righteous so that he knew just what to say in the *Jackson Daily News* when one of our fellow Mississippians had the unmitigated gall to publish, and expect other Mississippians to read, a book like *Sanctuary*.

Gypsy Smith may have been a Methodist; I don't know. At any rate, our Sunday school class was expected to attend, but I did not go up to be saved. Though all my life susceptible to anyone on a stage, I never would have been able to hold up my hand in front of the crowd at the City Auditorium and "come forward" while the choir leaned out singing "Come home! Come home! All God's children, come home, come home!" And I never felt anything like the pang of secular longing that I'd felt as a much younger child to go up onto the stage at the Century Theatre when the magician dazzlingly called for the valuable assistance of a child from the audience in the performance of his next feat of magic.

Neither was my father among the businessmen who were saved. As if the whole town were simply going through a temperamental meteorological disturbance, he remained calm and at home on Congress Street.

My mother did too. She liked reading her Bible in her own rocking chair, and while she rocked. She considered herself something of a student. "Run get me my Concordance," she'd say, referring to a little book bound in thin leather, falling apart. She liked to correct herself. Then from time to time her lips would twitch in the stern books of the Bible, such as Romans, providing her as they did with memories of her Grandfather Carden who had been a Baptist preacher in the days when she grew up in West Virginia. She liked to try in retrospect to correct Grandpa too.

I painlessly came to realize that the reverence I felt for

the holiness of life is not ever likely to be entirely at home in organized religion. It was later, when I was able to travel farther, that the presence of holiness and mystery seemed, as far as my vision was able to see, to descend into the windows of Chartres, the stone peasant figures in the capitals of Autun, the tall sheets of gold on the walls of Torcello that reflected the light of the sea; in the frescoes of Piero, of Giotto; in the shell of a church wall in Ireland still standing on a floor of sheep-cropped grass with no ceiling other than the changing sky.

I'm grateful that, from my mother's example, I had found the base for this worship—that I had found a love of sitting and reading the Bible for myself and looking up things in it.

How many of us, the South's writers-to-be of my generation, were blessed in one way or another, if not blessed alike, in not having gone deprived of the King James Version of the Bible. Its cadence entered into our ears and our memories for good. The evidence, or the ghost of it, lingers in all our books.

"In the beginning was the Word."

After Sunday school, Daddy might take us children to visit his office. The Lamar Life was in those days housed in a little one-story four-columned Greek temple, next door to the Pythian Castle—a building with crenellations and a high roof that looked as though Douglas Fairbanks might come swinging out of the top window on a rope. On Sunday, nobody else was in Daddy's building, and the water in the cooler was dead quiet too, warm and flat. There was a low mahogany fence around his office with a little gate for people to enter by, and he let us swing on his gate and bounce on the leather davenport while he went over his mail. He put the earphones over my ears to let me discover what I could hear on his dictaphone (I believe he had the first in Jackson). I heard his voice speaking to Miss Montgomery; this was his secretary, who always wore her hair in stylish puffs over her ears, and I had seen her seated at her typewriter while wearing these earphones right on top of her puffs.

He allowed us all our turns to peck at the typewriter. We used the Lamar Life stationery, which carried on its letterhead an oval portrait of Lucius Quintus Cincinnatus Lamar, for whom the Company had been named: a Mississippian who had been a member of Congress, Secretary of the Interior under Cleveland, and a U.S. Supreme Court Justice, a powerful orator who had pressed for the better reconciliation of North and South after the Civil War. Under his bearded portrait we all wrote letters to Mother.

She kept one of Walter's. There wasn't much of it he could spell, but it said, to help her guess who had written it, "Dear Mrs. C. W. Welty. I think you know me. I think you like me."

I can't think I had much of a sense of humor as long as I remained the only child. When my brother Edward came along after I was three, we both became comics, making each other laugh. We set each other off, as we did for life, from the minute he learned to talk. A sense of the absurd was communicated between us probably before that.

Though he hated to see me reading to myself, he accepted my reading to him as long as it made him laugh. We read the same things over and over, chapters from *Alice,* stretches from *Tom Sawyer,* Edward Lear's "Story of the Four Little Children Who Went Around the World." Whenever we came to the names of the four little children we rang them out in unison—"Violet, Slingsby, Guy, and Lionel!" And fell over. We kept this up at mealtimes, screaming nonsense at each other. My mother would warn us that we were *acting* the fool and would very shortly be asked to leave the table. She wouldn't call one of us a fool, or allow us to do it either. "He who calleth his brother a fool," she'd interrupt us, "is in danger of hell fire." I think she never in her life called anyone a fool, though she never bore one gladly, but she *would* say, "Well, it appears to me that Mrs. So-and-So is the least bit *limited.*"

Walter, three years again younger than Edward, was soberer than we. In his long baby dress he looked like a judge. I snatched up his baby bathtub and got behind it and danced for him, to hear him really crow. On the pink bottom of his tub I'd drawn a face with crayons, and all he could see of anybody's being there was my legs prancing under it. Walter wore a little kimono when he was up from acidosis, and, another way of adoring him, Edward tried to teach him to fly off Daddy's chair in his kimono, spreading the sleeves, then cried on the floor with him. Walter grew up to be the most serious in his expression of the three of us, and remained the calmest—the one who most took after our father.

When one of us caught measles or whooping cough and we were isolated in bed upstairs, we wrote notes to each other perhaps on the hour. Our devoted mother would pass them for us, after first running them in a hot oven to kill the germs. They came into our hands curled up and warm, sometimes scorched, like toast. Edward replied to my funny notes with his funny drawings. He was a born cartoonist.

In the Spanish influenza epidemic, when Edward had high fever in one room and I high fever in another, I shot him off a jingle about the little boy down our street who was in bed with the same thing: "There was a little boy and his name was Lindsey. He went to Heaven with the influenzy." My mother, horrified, told me to be ashamed of myself and refused to deliver it. So I saw we were all pretty sick, though a proper horror, on finding out what heedless written words of mine have really said, had to come later, as it has. But Edward and I and Lindsey all three got well, and so did Mother, who had much the worst case.

All children in those small-town, unhurried days had a vast inner life going on in the movies. Whole families attended together in the evenings, at least once a week, and children

49

were allowed to go without chaperone in the long summer afternoons—schoolmates with their best friends, pairs of little girls trotting on foot the short distance through the park to town under their Japanese parasols.

In devotion to Buster Keaton, Charlie Chaplin, Ben Blue, and the Keystone Kops, my brother Edward and I collapsed in laughter. My sense of making fictional comedy undoubtedly caught its first spark from the antic pantomime of the silent screen, and from having a kindred soul to laugh with.

The silent movies were a source also of words that you might never have learned anywhere else. You read them in the captions. "Jeopardy," for example, I got to know from *Drums of Jeopardy* with Alice Brady, who was wearing a leopard skin, a verbal connection I shall never forget. *The Cabinet of Dr. Caligari* turned up by some strange fluke in place of the Saturday western on the screen of the Istrione Theatre (known as the Eyestrain) where it was seen by an attendance consisting entirely of children. I learned "somnambulist" in terror, a word I still never hear or read without seeing again Conrad Veidt in black tights and bangs, making his way at night alongside a high leaning wall with eyes closed, one arm reaching high, seeing with his fingers. But of course all of us together in the movie had screamed with laughter, laughing at what terrified us, exactly as if it were funny, and exactly as grown-up audiences do today.

Events that weren't quite clear in meaning, things we children were shielded from, seemed to have their own routes, their own streets in town, and you might hear them coming near but then they never came, like the organ grinder with his monkey—surely you'd see him, but then the music went down the other street, and the monkey couldn't find you, though you waited with your penny.

In Davis School days, there lived a little boy two or three streets over from ours who was home sick in bed, and when the circus came to town that year, someone got the parade to march up a different street from the usual way to the Fairgrounds, to go past his house. He was carried to the window to watch it go by. Just for him the ponderous elephants, the plumes, the spangles, the acrobats, the clowns, the caged lion, the band playing, the steam calliope, the whole thing! When not long after that he disappeared forever from our view, having died of what had given him his special privilege, none of this at all was acceptable to the rest of us children. He had been tricked, not celebrated, by the parade's brazen marching up his street with the band playing, and we had somehow been tricked by envying him—betrayed into it.

It is not for nothing that an ominous feeling often attaches itself to a procession. This was when I learned it. "The Pied Piper of Hamelin" had done more than just hint at this. In films and stories we see spectacles forming in the street and parades coming from around the corner, and we know to greet them with distrust and apprehension: their intent is still to be revealed. (Think what it was in "My Kinsman, Major Molineux.")

I never resisted it when, in almost every story I ever wrote, some parade or procession, impromptu or ceremonious, comic or mocking or funereal, has risen up to mark some stage of the story's unfolding. They've started from far back.

We all had something like the same sense of humor. It was in losing our tempers that we were wide apart. Our tempers were all strong and intense. When we children quarreled, my brother Edward, in the terrible position of having to hit either a girl or a baby, yelled the loudest in outrage and was driven to bite. Walter, resourceful and practical in his childish fury as in everything else, was locked into the basement once by Edward who had grown tired of being followed around; but our little brother found the ax and made a good start on chopping himself a hole through the bottom of the door before rescue came.

I didn't hit other people or hit purposefully, I just hit. Some object would be at fault. In one case it was a pin-oak tree in the park which I had climbed all the way up and now couldn't get down. So I screamed and hit it with my head, the only part I could spare, and did my best to have a tantrum, while my family stood below making fun and arguing that nobody could bring me down but me. My anger was at myself, every time, all vanity. As an adolescent I was a slammer of drawers and a packer of suitcases. I was responsible for scenes.

Control came imperfectly to all of us: we reached it at

different times of life, frustrated, shot into indignation, by different things—some that are grown out of, and others not.

"I don't understand where you children *get* it," said my mother. "I never lose my temper. I just get hurt." (But that was it.)

One time, and one time only, she told us in a voice that opens a subject to close it, "I believe your father himself had a terrible temper once. But he learned to control his, a long time ago."

We tried to imagine Daddy swinging our ax. We could not, even our precious Walter, who had done it.

Of all my strong emotions, anger is the one least responsible for any of my work. I don't write out of anger. For one thing, simply as a fiction writer, I am minus an adversary—except, of course, that of time—and for another thing, the act of writing in itself brings me happiness.

There was one story that anger certainly lit the fuse of. In the 1960s, in my home town of Jackson, the civil rights leader Medgar Evers was murdered one night in darkness, and I wrote a story that same night about the murderer (his identity then unknown) called "Where Is the Voice Coming From?" But all that absorbed me, though it started as outrage, was the necessity I felt for entering into the mind and inside the skin of a character who could hardly have been more alien or repugnant to me. Trying for my utmost, I wrote it in the first person. I was wholly vaunting the prerogative of the short-story writer. It is always vaunting, of course, to imagine yourself inside another person, but it is what a story writer does in every piece of work; it is his first step, and his last too, I suppose. I'm not sure this story was brought off; and I don't believe that my anger showed me anything about human character that my sympathy and rapport never had.

Even as we grew up, my mother could not help imposing herself between her children and whatever it was they might take it in mind to reach out for in the world. For she would get it for them, if it was good enough for them—she would have to be very sure—and give it to them, at whatever cost to herself: valiance was in her very fibre. She stood always prepared in herself to challenge the world in our place. She did indeed tend to make the world look dangerous, and so it had been to her. A way had to be found around her love sometimes, without challenging *that*, and at the same time cherishing it in its unassailable strength. Each of us children did, sooner or later, in part at least, solve this in a different, respectful, complicated way.

But I think she was relieved when I chose to be a writer of stories, for she thought writing was safe.

II

Learning to See

II

Learning to See

When we set out in our five-passenger Oakland touring car on our summer trip to Ohio and West Virginia to visit the two families, my mother was the navigator. She sat at the alert all the way at Daddy's side as he drove, correlating the AAA Blue Book and the speedometer, often with the baby on her lap. She'd call out, "All right, Daddy: '86-point-2, crossroads. Jog right, past white church. Gravel ends.'—And there's the church!" she'd say, as though we had scored. Our road always became her adversary. "This doesn't surprise me at all," she'd say as Daddy backed up a mile or so into our own dust on a road that had petered out. "I could've told you a road that looked like that had little intention of going anywhere."

"It was the first one we'd seen all day going in the right direction," he'd say. His sense of direction was unassailable, and every mile of our distance was familiar to my father by rail. But the way we set out to go was popularly known as "through the country."

My mother's hat rode in the back with the children, suspended over our heads in a pillowcase. It rose and fell with us when we hit the bumps, thumped our heads and bat-

57

ted our ears in an authoritative manner when sometimes we bounced as high as the ceiling. This was 1917 or 1918; a lady couldn't expect to travel without a hat.

Edward and I rode with our legs straight out in front of us over some suitcases. The rest of the suitcases rode just outside the doors, strapped on the running boards. Cars weren't made with trunks. The tools were kept under the back seat and were heard from in syncopation with the bumps; we'd jump out of the car so Daddy could get them out and jack up the car to patch and vulcanize a tire, or haul out the tow rope or the tire chains. If it rained so hard we couldn't see the road in front of us, we waited it out, snapped in behind the rain curtains and playing "Twenty Questions."

My mother was not naturally observant, but she could scrutinize; when she gave the surroundings her attention, it was to verify something—the truth or a mistake, hers or another's. My father kept his eyes on the road, with glances toward the horizon and overhead. My brother Edward periodically stood up in the back seat with his eyelids fluttering while he played the harmonica, "Old Macdonald had a farm" and "Abdul the Bulbul Amir," and the baby slept in Mother's lap and only woke up when we crossed some rattling old bridge. "*There's* a river!" he'd crow to us all. "Why, it certainly *is*," my mother would reassure him, patting him back to sleep. I rode as a hypnotic, with my set gaze on the landscape that vibrated past at twenty-five miles an hour. We were all wrapped by the long ride into some cocoon of our own.

Learning to See

The journey took about a week each way, and each day had my parents both in its grip. Riding behind my father I could see that the road had him by the shoulders, by the hair under his driving cap. It took my mother to make him stop. I inherited his nervous energy in the way I can't stop writing on a story. It makes me understand how Ohio had him around the heart, as West Virginia had my mother. Writers and travelers are mesmerized alike by knowing of their destinations.

And all the time that we think we're getting there so fast, how slowly we do move. In the days of our first car trip, Mother proudly entered in her log, "Mileage today: 161!" with an exclamation mark.

"A Detroit car passed us yesterday." She always kept those logs, with times, miles, routes of the day's progress, and expenses totaled up.

That kind of travel made you conscious of borders; you rode ready for them. Crossing a river, crossing a county line, crossing a state line—especially crossing the line you couldn't see but knew was there, between the South and the North—you could draw a breath and feel the difference.

The Blue Book warned you of the times for the ferries to run; sometimes there were waits of an hour between. With rivers and roads alike winding, you had to cross some rivers three times to be done with them. Lying on the water at the foot of a river bank would be a ferry no bigger than somebody's back porch. When our car had been driven on board—often it was down a roadless bank, through sliding

59

stones and runaway gravel, with Daddy simply aiming at the two-plank gangway—father and older children got out of the car to enjoy the trip. My brother and I got barefooted to stand on wet, sun-warm boards that, weighted with your car, seemed exactly on the level with the water; our feet were the same as in the river. Some of these ferries were operated by a single man pulling hand over hand on a rope bleached and frazzled as if made from cornshucks.

I watched the frayed rope running through his hands. I thought it would break before we could reach the other side.

"No, it's not going to break," said my father. "It's never broken before, has it?" he asked the ferry man.

"No sirree."

"You see? If it never broke before, it's not going to break this time."

His general belief in life's well-being worked either way. If you had a pain, it was "Have you ever had it before? You have? It's not going to kill you, then. If you've had the same thing before, you'll be all right in the morning."

My mother couldn't have more profoundly disagreed with that.

"You're such an optimist, dear," she often said with a sigh, as she did now on the ferry.

"You're a good deal of a pessimist, sweetheart."

"I certainly *am*."

And yet I was well aware as I stood between them with the water running over my toes, he the optimist was the one who was prepared for the worst, and she the pessimist was the daredevil: he the one who on our trip carried chains and a coil of rope and an ax all upstairs to our hotel bedroom every night in case of fire, and she the one—before I was born—when there *was* a fire, had broken loose from all hands and run back—on crutches, too—into the burning house to rescue her set of Dickens which she flung, all twenty-four volumes, from the window before she jumped out after them, all for Daddy to catch.

"I make no secret of my lifelong fear of the water," said my mother, who on ferry boats remained inside the car, clasping the baby to her—my brother Walter, who was destined to prowl the waters of the Pacific Ocean in a minesweeper.

As soon as the sun was beginning to go down, we went more slowly. My father would drive sizing up the towns, inspecting the hotel in each, deciding where we could safely spend the night. Towns little or big had beginnings and ends, they reached to an edge and stopped, where the country began again as though they hadn't happened. They were intact and to themselves. You could see a town lying ahead in its whole, as definitely formed as a plate on a table. And your road entered and ran straight through the heart of it; you could see it all, laid out for your passage through. Towns, like people, had clear identities and your imagination could go out to meet them. You saw houses, yards, fields, and people busy in them, the people that had a life where they were.

You could hear their bank clocks striking, you could smell their bakeries. You would know those towns again, recognize the salient detail, seen so close up. Nothing was blurred, and in passing along Main Street, slowed down from twenty-five to twenty miles an hour, you didn't miss anything on either side. Going somewhere "through the country" acquainted you with the whole way there and back.

My mother never fully gave in to her pleasure in our trip—for pleasure every bit of it was to us all—because she knew we were traveling with a loaded pistol in the pocket on the door of the car on Daddy's side. I doubt if my father fired off any kind of gun in his life, but he could not have carried his family from Jackson, Mississippi, to West Virginia and Ohio through the country, unprotected.

This was not the first time I'd been brought here to visit Grandma in West Virginia, but the first visit I barely remembered. Where I stood now was inside the house where my mother had been born and where she grew up. It was a low, gray-weathered wooden house with a broad hall through the middle of it with the light of day at each end, the house that Ned Andrews, her father, had built to stand on the very top of the highest mountain he could find.

"And here's where I first began to read my Dickens," Mother said, pointing. "Under that very bed. Hiding my candle. To keep them from knowing what I was up to all night."

"But where did it all *come* from?" I asked her at last. "All that Dickens?"

"Why, Papa gave me that set of Dickens for agreeing to let them cut off my hair," she said, as if surprised that a reason like that wouldn't have occurred to me. "In those days, they thought very long thick hair like mine would sap a child's strength. I said *No!* I wanted my hair left the very way it was. They offered me gold earrings first—in those days little girls often developed a wish to have their ears pierced and fitted with little gold rings. I said *No!* I'd rather keep my hair. Then Papa said, 'What about books? I'll have them send a whole set of Charles Dickens to you, right up the river from Baltimore, in a barrel.' I agreed."

Ned Andrews had been the county's youngest member of the bar. He quickly made a name for himself on the side as an orator. When he gave the dedicatory address for the opening of a new courthouse in Nicholas County, West Virginia, my mother put away a copy. He is praising the architecture of the building: "The student turns with a sigh of relief from the crumbling pillars and columns of Athens and Alexandria to the symmetrical and colossal temples of the New World. As time eats from the tombstones of the past the epitaphs of primeval greatness, and covers the pyramids with the moss of forgetfulness, she directs the eye to the new temples of art and progress that make America the monumental beacon-light of the world."

People may have expected the highfalutin in oratory in

those days, but they might not have expected Ned's courtroom flair. There was a murder trial of a woman given to fortunetelling. She had been overheard reading in an old man's cards that his days were numbered. When, the very next day, this old man had been found in his bed dead from a gunshot wound, it appeared to the public that that fortuneteller might have known too much about it. She was put on trial for murder. Ned Andrews' defense centered on the well-known fact that the old man kept his loaded gun mounted at all times over the head of his bed. This was the gun that had shot him. The old man could have discharged it perfectly easily himself, Ned argued, by carelessly bouncing on the bed a little bit. He proposed to prove it, and invited the jury of dubious mountaineers to watch him do it. Leading them all the way up the mountain to the old man's cabin, he mounted the gun in place on its rests, having first loaded it with blank shells, and while they watched he mimicked the old man and made a running jump onto the bed. The gun jarred loose, tumbled down, and fired at him. He rested his case. The fortuneteller was without any more ado declared not guilty.

He was brim full of talents. He'd attended Trinity College (later, Duke University) where he organized a literary society; he'd been a journalist and a photographer in Norfolk, Virginia, and in West Virginia where he'd run away to, to seek adventure, he'd turned into a lawyer. He seems to have been a legendary fisherman in those mountain streams, is still now and then referred to in local sportsmen's tales. Ned was impervious to the sting of bees and could always be summoned to capture a wild swarm. Ned was the one they sent for when someone fell down an empty well, because he was not afraid to harness himself and be lowered into the deathly gasses at the bottom and bring the unconscious victim up again.

Yet the human failings Mother could least forgive in other people, she regarded with only tenderness in him. I gathered—slowly and over the years I gathered—that sometimes he drank. He told tall tales to his wife, Eudora Carden. He told one to begin with, in order to marry her, saying he was of age to do so, when he was nineteen and four years younger than she. She was superstitious; he loved to tease her with tricks, to stage elaborate charades with the connivance of one of his little boys, that preyed on her fear of ghosts. He shocked her with a tale—Mother said there was nothing to prove it wasn't a fact—that one of the Andrews ancestors had been hanged in Ireland. Eudora Carden came from the home of a strongly dedicated Baptist preacher, and about all preachers he was irreverent and irrepressible. I have seen photographs he took of her—tintypes; it's clear that he took them with great care to show how beautiful he found her. In one she is standing up behind a chair, with her long hands crossed at the wrist over the back of it; she is dressed in her best, with her dark hair drawn high above her oval face and tucked with a flower that looks like a wild rose.

She is very young. She has long gray eyes over high cheek-bones; she is gazing to the front, looking straight at him. Her mouth is sensitive, her lips youthfully full. She told her daughter Chessie years later that she was objecting to his taking this picture because she was pregnant at the time, and the pose—the crossed hands on the back of a chair—had been to hide that. (With my mother herself, I wondered, her first child?) When she came back from the well on cold mornings, her hands would be bleeding from breaking the ice on it: this is what my mother would remember when she looked at those soft hands in the tintypes.

I don't know from whom it came or to whom it was passed, but at one time an old, home-made drawing of the Andrews family tree came into my mother's hands. It was rolled up; if unrolled it was capable of rattling shut the next instant. The tree was drawn as a living tree, spreading from a rooted trunk, every branch, twig, and leaf in clear outline, all with names and dates on them in a copperplate handwriting. The most riveting feature was the thick branch stemming from near the base of the main trunk: it was broken off short to a jagged end, branchless and leafless, and labeled "Joseph, Killed by lightning."

It had been executed with the finest possible pen in ink grown very pale, as if it had been drawn in watered maple syrup. The leaves weren't stiffly drawn or conventional ellipses, all alike, but each one daintily fashioned with a pointed tip and turned on its stem this way or that, as if this family tree were tossed by a slight breeze. The massed whole had the look, at that time to me, of a children's puzzle in which you were supposed to find your mother. I found mine—only a tiny leaf on a twig of a branch near the top, hardly big enough to hold her tiny name.

The Andrews branch my mother came from represents the mix most usual in the Southeast—English, Scottish, Irish, with a dash of French Huguenot. The first American one, Isham, who fought in the Revolutionary War, was born in Virginia and moved to Georgia, where succeeding generations lived. The Andrewses were not a rural clan, like the Weltys; they lived in towns, were educators and preachers, with some Methodist circuit riders; one cousin of Ned's (Walter Hines Page) was an ambassador to England. Trinity College educated some of them, including, for an impatient time, young Ned. By the time my mother's father, Edward Raboteau Andrews (Ned) was born in 1862, the family had returned to Virginia. He broke from the mold and at eighteen ran away from a home of parents, grandparents, sisters, brothers, and aunts in Norfolk to become the first West Virginian.

Here in the center of the Andrews kitchen, at the same long table where the family always ate, not too far from where Grandma seemed to be always busy at the warm stove, Ned had sat and worked up his cases for the defense in Clay Courthouse, far below and out of sight straight down the mountain. Mother remembered him transposing band music there, too; he had sent off for the instruments, got together a band, and proceeded to teach them to play in concert, lined up on the courthouse lawn: he had a strong need of music. His children had an instrument to learn to play too: he assigned my mother the cornet. (When I think back to how she sang "Blessed Assurance" while washing the dishes, I realize she flatted her high notes just where a child's cornet might.)

It was in the quilted bed in the front room of this house where he lay in so much pain (probably from the affliction that brought on his death, an infected appendix) that he once told Mother, a little girl, to bring the kitchen knife and plunge it into his side; she, hypnotized, almost believed she must obey. It was from that door that later she went with him on the frozen winter night when it was clear he had to get, somehow, to a hospital. The mountain roads were impassable, there was ice in the Elk River: but a neighbor vowed he could make way by raft. She was fifteen. Leaving her mother and the five little brothers at home, Chessie went with him. Her father lay on the raft, on which a fire had been lit to warm him, Chessie beside him. The neighbor managed to pole the raft through the icy river and eventually across it to a railroad. They flagged the train. (It seems likely that the place they flagged it was the same as where my mother and I were let off that train when I was three, arriving on that nearly forgotten visit. It was an early summer dawn; everything was a cloud of mist—we were standing on the bank of a river and I didn't know it. When my mother pulled the rope of an iron bell, we watched a boat come out of the mist to meet us, with her five brothers all inside.)

Mother had to return by herself from Baltimore, her father's body in a coffin on the same train. He had died on the operating table in Johns Hopkins, of a ruptured appendix, at thirty-seven years of age. The last lucid remark he'd made to my mother was "If you let them tie me down, I'll die." (The surgeon had come out where she stood waiting in the hall. "Little girl," he'd said, "you'd better get in touch now with somebody in Baltimore." "Sir, I don't know anybody in Baltimore," she said, and what she never forgot was his astounded reply: "You don't know anybody in *Baltimore*?")

It was from this house that my mother very soon after that piled up her hair and went out to teach in a one-room school, mountain children little and big alike. The first day, some fathers came along to see if she could whip their children, some who were older than she. She told the children that she did intend to whip them if they became unruly and refused to learn, and invited the fathers to stay if they liked and she'd be able to whip them too. Having been thus tried out, she was a great success with them after that. She left home every day on her horse; since she had the river to cross, a little brother rode on her horse behind her, to ride him home, while she rowed across the river in a boat. And he would be there to meet her with her horse again at evening. All this way, to pass the time, she told me, she recited the poems in McGuffey's Readers out loud.

She could still recite them in full when she was lying helpless and nearly blind, in her bed, an old lady. Reciting, her voice took on resonance and firmness, it rang with the old fervor, with ferocity even. She was teaching me one more, almost her last, lesson: emotions do not grow old. I knew that I would feel as she did, and I do.

Teaching, my mother earned, little by little, money enough to go to nearby Marshall College in the summers and in time was graduated. Her mind was filled with *Paradise Lost*, she told me later, showing me the notebook she still kept with its diagrams. It was as a schoolteacher she'd met my father, Christian Welty, a young man from Ohio, who had come to work that summer in the office of a lumber company in the vicinity. While they courted, they used to take long walks up and down the railroad tracks, which I imagine my father found in themselves romantic—they took snapshots of each other, my father with one foot on a milepost, my mother sitting on a stile with an open book and wearing a "fascinator" over her hair. My father had her snap his picture standing on a moving sidecar, his hand at the lever. It was in leaving this house that she married him and set off for a new life and a new part of the world for both of them, in Jackson, Mississippi.

Mother's brothers were called "the boys." Their long-necked banjos hung on pegs along the wide hall, as casually as hats and coats. Coming in from outdoors, Carl and Mose lifted their banjos off the wall and sat down side by side and struck in. This was what I remembered from my early visit; I had till now forgotten. They played together like soulmates. At age three, I'd cried "Two Carls!" They sang in the same perfect beat, perfect unison, "Frog Went A-Courting and He Did Ride."

That effortless, drumlike rhythm, heard in double, too, would have put a claim on any child. They had a repertoire of ballads and country songs and rousing hymns. My mother would tell her brothers, plead with them, to stop—I didn't want to go to bed. "Aw, Sister, let Girlie have her one more song," and one song could keep going without loss of a beat into still one more.

The boys liked to sing together too, all five, without accompaniment. Gus, the heaviest, with his broad chest, dominated the others with a bass down to his toes. Those old hymns they'd grown up with, coming out chorus after chorus, sounded more and more uproarious, especially sung outdoors. "Roll, Jordan, Roll" would fill the air around them and roll back on them from the next mountain in echoes, as if the mountain were full of singers like blackbirds in a pie, just waiting for the song to let them out.

I don't suppose now that my mother ever thought of her father in any other light than the one she saw him in when she was a little girl—for he didn't live much beyond then. All I was given to know of him myself is her same childlike vision, uncorrectable—half of it adoring dream, half brutal

71

memory of his death, the part of his story that she, all by herself, was the one able to tell. Her brothers were all too little to have kept a clear memory of him at all; they remembered his songs best, remembered him when *they* sang, and told how he made up more and more verses to "Where Have You Been, Billy Boy?" putting his own rambunctious words to the tune. What they remember is what the stories tell about him, and what they could see lay in their mother.

What did my father, Christian Welty, think of all these stories of her father my mother told? I never knew. My father was his very opposite, all that was stable, reticent, self-contained, willing to be patient if need be, and, in all *he* said, factual. Before the birth of my brothers, when my mother and I went up on the train alone, my father would come at the end of our visit to shepherd us home. Perhaps I remembered this without too much understanding, but I was not too much of a baby to notice and remember how different it was when my father arrived on the scene. A difference came over whatever we were doing, like a change in the wind.

The fact was my mother and I were the only ones really dying to see him come. Of course he was older than they, the brothers—six years older than Chessie, their older sister—and he was a Yankee, but I came to realize later what must have been the real reason for the polite distance they put into their welcome: ever since he'd first come courting, they'd known he was only here to take their sister away from them.

It was in this house they saw their sister married. Mother's brothers never in my memory called my father other than "Mr. Welty," and certainly they didn't then, on their wedding day; Moses, the youngest, went out and "cried on the ground." The newlyweds left on the train for the World's Fair and Louisiana Purchase Centennial Exposition that had opened (a year late) in St. Louis. It was October 1904. They would then go on to Jackson, Mississippi, and the future. My mother thought it was ill-becoming to brag about your courage; the nearest she came was to say, "Yes, I expect I was pretty venturesome."

It must have seemed to her family behind her that she had been cut off from them forever. They never really got over her absence from home.

I don't think she ever really got over it either. I think she could listen sometimes and hear the mountain's voice—the delayed echo of the unseen and distant old man—"just an old hermit," said Grandma—chopping wood with his ax and calling on God in alternation, in answering blows; the prattling of the Queen's Shoals in Elk River somewhere below, equally out of sight, which I believed I could hear from Grandma's front-yard rocking chair, though I was told that I must be listening to something else; the loss and recovery of traveling sound, the *carrying* of the voice that called as if on long threads the hand could hold to, so I would keep asking who that was, who was still out of sight but calling in the mountains as he neared us, as we brought him near.

I think when my mother came to Jackson she brought

West Virginia with her. Of course, I brought some of it with me too.

For as long as she lived, letters went back and forth every day between my grandmother and my mother. Grandma always had to concern herself with her letters getting carried down the mountain to the Court House to make the train.

Dear Chessie, I wrote to you last night but did not give it to Gus this morning as I thought Carl would be sure to go to the C.H. and as he had letters of his own to mail would not be likely to forget. He had his overcoat on to go before dinner but I told him that dinner was ready and after we had started to eat Moses came in and said the dog was after a fox and all of the boys left as soon as they were through dinner and here is my letter and I hear the train now so it will not go. It stopped raining last night and today it has been snowing part of the time and blowing nearly all of the time and so dark and gloomy looking that I only sit by the fire. I wish you had a half dozen of my chickens. I killed three last week for the boys to take to school. I do wish I could step in a while and see you and as I cannot I think I will take a nap. With lots of love from Mother.

and

. . . Carl is writing letters to different ones that he thinks might come to school, Gus and Moses are playing on their banjoes as Eudora would say, I do not know what John is

doing, he is in the other room . . . Say, do you believe that two pigeons could be sent from here to Eudora say in April or do you think they could not go without some one being along to take care of them. She would like them for they would fly all around her and eat out of her hand if she would let them. We are all well and do hope you are all well, with lots of love from Mother, and kiss Baby.

and one on a November 4:

My dear child, I received no letter yesterday but had expected to start one to you this morning but failed. I had thought I would walk to the C.H. and started to get ready. It is a beautiful day overhead, you cannot see a cloud and yet the wind is fearful. I have nearly finished my looming [?], scrubbed the dining room and kitchen, picked up three or four bushels of walnuts, I washed yesterday and found two hen's nests with sixteen eggs in them. I told Gus I had saved 75¢ or a dollar and made a quarter, as eggs are 25¢ a dozen . . . The boys have started to school and I believe they will learn, they both seem pleased with their Teacher. Maggie Keeney's fourth sister is teaching the lower room. Maggie Cora and Mattie as you may know are married, that leaves Hester and this one to teach. Gus said last night that one of Clay's teachers died yesterday, a bright young man. I wish I was able to do with my hands as fast as I find jobs to do, and maybe I could set things straight but I cannot do that. I am lonely enough but if you and baby could walk in sometime to see Grandma I would do all right but I hope both and all three of you keep well, with a heart full of love from Mother.

This is a letter she wrote to me:

My dear Eudora Alice, I do wish I could go on the choo choo train and see you and be at your little party, I would bring you two pretty little pigeons, for I know both you and your little friends would enjoy having them, but as I cannot go nor send the little pigeons, I am going to the Court House this morning and see if I can send you a little cup of sugar you can eat and think of Grandma. I hope you will have a nice time and be well. With lots of love from Grandma. P.S. Tell your Ma I will write to her next time.

Such were my mother's component parts.

Grandma had thought my agitation and apprehension of her over-familiar pigeons was love. I can see now that perhaps she was right.

That summer, lying in the long grass with my head propped against the back of a saddle, with the zenith above me and the drop of distance below, I listened to the mountain silence until I could hear as far into it as the faintest clink of a cowbell. In the mountains, what might be out of sight had never really gone away. Like the mountain, that distant bell would always be there. It would keep reminding.

• • •

It took the mountain top, it seems to me now, to give me the sensation of independence. It was as if I'd discovered something I'd never tasted before in my short life. Or rediscovered it—for I associated it with the taste of the water that came out of the well, accompanied with the ring of that long metal sleeve against the sides of the living mountain, as from deep down it was wound up to view brimming and streaming long drops behind it like bright stars on a ribbon. It thrilled me to drink from the common dipper. The coldness, the far, unseen, unheard springs of what was in my mouth now, the iron strength of its flavor that drew my cheeks in, its fern-laced smell, all said mountain mountain mountain as I swallowed. Every swallow was making me a part of being here, sealing me in place, with my bare feet planted on the mountain and sprinkled with my rapturous spills. What I felt I'd come here to do was something on my own.

My mother adored her brothers, "the boys," and she was their heart. One day she and the boys, taking me along, were dawdling down the mountain path and talking family together. I thought I'd take off on a superior track I saw for myself, and the next moment I was flying down it, straight down, then falling, rolling and tumbling, gathering dust and leaves in my clothes and hair, and I could hear a long rip coming in my skirt without being able to stop until some bush caught hold of me. I got to my feet and looked back up. It wasn't far, but my mother and the boys might have been standing over the rim of the moon: they were laughing at me, my mother along with the boys, helplessly laughing. One of my uncles dropped down to me and carried me up again. I went back with them, riding on his shoulders. The boys, though not my mother now, were still teasing, and I was aloft up there, hanging my head or holding it up—I can't be sure now.

"Well, now Girlie's learned what a log chute is," said Uncle Carl, putting me down in front of Grandma as if to let her in on the family joke. Her gesture then was the last other thing I remembered from being here before: with her fore-finger she pushed my hair behind my ears and bared my face to hers. She looked seriously right into my eyes. Hadn't we come right to the point of our both being named Eudora?

"Run take that little dress of yours off, and Grandma'll sew up the hole in it right quick," she said. Then she looked from me to my mother and back. I learned on our trip what that look meant: it was matching family faces.

The Cardens had been in West Virginia for a while—I believe were there before West Virginia was a state. Eudora Carden's own mother had been Eudora Ayres, of an Orange County, Virginia, family, the daughter of a Huguenot mother and an English father. He was a planter, fairly well-to-do. Eudora Ayres married another young Virginian, William Carden, who was poor and called a "dreamer"; and when these two innocents went to start life in the wild mountainous country, in the unknown part that had separated itself from Virginia, among his possessions he brought his leather-covered Latin dictionary and grammar, and she brought her father's wedding present of five slaves. The dictionary was forever kept in the tiny farmhouse and the slaves were let go. One of the stark facts of their lives in Enon is that during the Civil War Great-Grandfather Carden was taken prisoner and incarcerated in Ohio on suspicion of being, as a Virginian, a Confederate sympathizer, and lost his eyesight in confinement.

Their son, Mother's Grandpa Carden, was a Baptist preacher. Enon-near-Gilboa was the name of his church—taken from the Bible, of course; Gilboa, on the mountain as in the Bible, was the older church it was near to. This was where Eudora Carden and four brothers were born, and where later the Andrews children spent a great deal of their time. He was an enormously strict and vigorous-minded old man.

When his first wife died, leaving him a young man with little children, Grandpa did what so many did then: he sent back to Virginia for her sister. Then, after an interval, he married her. My mother, at a young and knowing age, once praised her to her face for her unselfishness in coming from Virginia and marrying Grandpa for the sake of his motherless children, and the old lady replied tartly, "Who says that's why I married him?"

My mother and the boys spent a lot of time visiting

Grandpa and Grandma Carden. This good old man liked to retire to the barn to say his bedtime prayers, where he could thunder them up as he pleased, to the rafters. Mother's little brothers used to delight in hiding in the hay where they could listen to Grandpa pray, and he on his side would be sure to get all their names in when he was asking for forgiveness and beg the Lord to be patient with them, whatever had been their sinful ways, and lead them into righteousness *before it was too late.*

Sometimes at our house, when my mother read the Bible in her rocking chair by the fire, she'd hail a passage to read out oratorically. "I'm just so strongly reminded of Grandpa Carden when I come to Romans," she'd say.

She'd been pretty lively toward Grandpa in her own youth. "I don't agree with Saint Paul," she'd told him once: it was in connection with the rule of wearing a hat to church.

In our picture of Grandpa Carden, his long beard and side whiskers are pure white, and seem to be stirred by some mountain wind. His large black hat is resting upside-down on his knee as he sits on a straight-back bench. His right hand is holding, straight up and down and thin as a rod, his staff; it looks four or five feet tall. The photograph is inscribed across the back in a strict hand, "To Chessie, if she will have it."

Those had been early days. I tend to think that it had been Ned Andrews who saw himself in West Virginia as some original pioneer; he was the lone romantic in this story. He might have delighted in imagining the figure he'd cut to them back in Tidewater Virginia. (They *did* wonder at him: I grew to know the Virginia kin, his remarkable mother and his sisters who, when they knew, rallied around young Chessie and all Ned's family.)

His fine-grained wife lived on as a woman of unceasing courage and of considerable grace, with a great deal to make the best of. In the eyes of all their devoted children, and in every word I ever heard them say, it appeared that neither of their parents could ever have done conscious wrong or made an irretrievable mistake in their lives. When their mother died, the boys came down from the mountain. They married and made their own lives—except for John, who died of pneumonia after enlisting in the Army in 1918—in teaching, banking, civic or business affairs below. Carl became mayor of Charleston. They never let go of the home place. It was kept up as a family retreat, a camp for hunting and fishing. My mother and her brothers were able to visit each other, not only in times of trouble or crisis. It became comparatively easy, one day, after all.

It seems likely to me now that the very element in my character that took possession of me there on top of the mountain, the fierce independence that was suddenly mine, to remain inside me no matter how it scared me when I tumbled, was an inheritance. Indeed it was my chief inheritance from my mother, who was braver. Yet, while she knew that independent spirit so well, it was what she so agonizingly tried to protect me from, in effect to warn me against. It was what we shared, it made the strongest bond between us and the strongest tension. To grow up is to fight for it, to grow old is to lose it after having possessed it. For her, too, it was most deeply connected to the mountains.

When she was old, widowed, ill, and losing her sight, my mother one day announced to me she would be very glad to have the piano back in our house. It was the Steinway upright she had bought for me when I was nine, so far beyond her means, and had paid for herself out of the housekeeping money, which she added to by buying a Jersey cow, milking her, and selling part of the milk to the neighbors on our street, in quart bottles which I delivered on my bicycle. While I sat on the piano stool practicing my scales, I imagined my mother sitting on her stool in the cowshed, her fingers just as rhythmically pulling the teats of Daisy.

Two of her children had played this piano, I practicing my lessons and my brother Edward all along playing better by ear. When her grand-daughters came along, the piano was sent to their house to practice their lessons on. Now, all those years later, Mother wanted it under her roof again. Right now! It was brought and, the same day, tuned. She asked me to go directly to it and play for her "The West Virginia Hills."

I sat down and remembered how it went, and as I played I heard her singing it—singing it to herself, just as she used to while washing the dishes after supper:

Learning to See

O the West Virginia hills!
How my heart with rapture thrills . . .
O the hills! Beautiful hills! . . .

This one moment seemed to satisfy her. Once from her wheelchair, afterwards, she tried to pick it out herself, laying her finger slowly down on keys she couldn't really see. "A mountaineer," she announced to me proudly, as though she had never told me this before and now I had better remember it, "always will be *free.*"

"Oh yes, we're in the North now," said my mother after we'd crossed the state line from West Virginia into Ohio. "The barns are all bigger than the houses. They care more about the horses and cows than they do about——" She forbore to say.

The farm my father grew up on, where Grandpa Welty and Grandma lived, was in southern Ohio in the rolling hills of Hocking County, near the small town of Logan. It was one of the neat, narrow-porched, two-story farmhouses, painted white, of the Pennsylvania-German country. Across its front grew feathery cosmos and barrel-sized peony bushes with stripy heavy-scented blooms pushing out of the leaves. There was a springhouse to one side, down a little walk only one brick in width, and an old apple orchard in front, the barn and the pasture and fields of corn and wheat behind. Periodically there came sounds from the barn, and you could hear the crows, but everything else was still.

In the house it was solid stillness, it seemed to me, at almost any hour, all day, except for dinnertime. Whoever was in the house seemed to remain invisible, but this was because they were all busy. I think in retrospect that my father had set our visit in time to help with the harvest, and certainly he was very busy outside all day. He let my brother Edward go with him.

My mother, in the way she had, never put aside her *first* impression of Grandpa Welty. She was hurt when he had met the train in the spring wagon, not the buggy. All the way home to the farm, he never started a conversation with her. "But that was his *custom*," years later she explained to me. "He never brought out much to say till I was ready to go. Then on my last day, on the long ride to the station, he never stopped talking at all. He talked up one blue streak." They took to each other enormously.

Throughout our visit, as long as the daylight held, he was out stirring about the barn or moving through the fields. He was a quiet, gentle man, with a flourishing mustache, with not much to say to the women and children in his house; when he did sit down, it would be in his wooden platform swing outside, usually with his pipe and holding one of the farm kittens on his knee. Now and then he held me there, and then I could hold the kitten.

My grandmother Welty was my father's stepmother. My mother would remark, "There's one thing I will have to say about Mother Welty: she makes the best *bread* I ever put in

84

my mouth." It really is the only thing I can remember she ever said about Grandma Welty, though she did feel often compelled to repeat it, and never said anything different after the old lady died.

Grandma Welty, with each work day in the week set firmly aside for a single task, was not very expectant of conversation either. Of course I remember Friday best—baking day. Her pies, enough for a week, were set to cool when done on the kitchen windowsills, side by side like so many cheeky faces telling us "One at a time!"

Like the hub that would make the dinner table go round, if it ever could start, was a tulip-shaped glass in the center in which the bright-polished teaspoons, all the largest family could ever need, stood facing in with their backs turned. I don't believe this spoonholder ever left the table. Even in the dark diningroom at midnight in the sleeping house, it would stand ready there. The smell of all those loaves of bread and the row of pies didn't easily go away either. And in the parlor where the blinds were drawn, the smell of being unvisited would pervade, pervade, pervade.

Compared to the Andrews clan, the Welty family at the time of the first visit I remember was very scarce in the way of uncles and cousins and kin of an older generation. Grandpa, Jefferson Welty, had been the youngest of thirteen children, but he is the only one I ever saw; his parents were Christian and Salome Welty, early settlers in Marion Township, Hocking County. The Weltys were originally German

Swiss; the first ones to come to this country, back before the Revolutionary War here, were three brothers, and the whole family is descended from them, I understand—it seems to hark back to German fairy-tale tradition.

My father is not the one who told me this: he never happened to tell us a single family story; could it have been because he'd heard so many of the Andrews stories? I think it was rather because, as he said, he had no interest in ancient history—only the future, he said, should count. At the same time, he was exceedingly devoted to his father, went to see him whenever he could, and wrote to him regularly from his desk at home; I grew up familiar with seeing the long envelopes being addressed in my father's clear, careful hand: Jefferson Welty, Esquire. It was the only use my father made of the word; he saved it for his father. I took "Esquire" for a term of reverence, and I think it stood for that with him; we were always aware that Daddy loved him.

An English Welti, who spelled his name thus with an *i*, wrote to me once from Kent, in curiosity, after an early book of mine had appeared over there; he asked me about my name. My father, who had never told us anything, had died, and this was before my mother set herself as she did later to looking into records. Mr. Welti knew about the whole throng of them, from medieval times on, and the three brothers who set forth to the New World from German Switzerland and settled from Virginia westward over Pennsylvania, Ohio, and Indiana before the Revolutionary

War. "I expect you know," wrote the British Mr. Welti, "that one unfortunate Welty fell at Saratoga."

The only part of his letter that would have interested my father is that about the St. Gotthard Tunnel and the Welty who pushed it through. The fact that this same Welty had been President of Switzerland seven times running would have caused him to say "Pshaw!," his strongest expletive. (That my mother's strongest exclamation was "Pshaw!" too rather took away some of its force for both of them.)

In Grandpa and Grandma's parlor stood the organ, which, my mother had whispered to me, they preferred not to hear played. I tiptoed around it as if it were asleep. There were steep, uphill pedals; the flowered carpet continued right on up them as if they were part of the floor. When opened, the organ gave off a smell sharp as an exclamation, as if opening it were a mistake in company manners, which I already knew. I chilled my finger by touching a key. The key did not yield. The whole keyboard withstood me as if it had been a kitchen table; I suppose the organ had to be pumped.

But either I had been told, or I got the feeling there and then that this organ had belonged to my father's real mother, who had died when he was a little boy. But when I was named Eudora for my Andrews grandmother, I had been named for this grandmother too. Alice was my middle name. Her name had been Allie. Too late, after I was already christened, it came out that Allie stood for not Alice but Almira. Her name had been remembered wrong. I imagined what that would have done to her. It seemed to me to have made her an orphan. That was worse to me than if I had been able to imagine dying.

Barefooted on the slick brick walk I rushed to where I could breathe in the cool breath from the interior of the springhouse. On a cold bubbling spring, covered dishes and crocks and pitchers of butter and milk and so on floated in a circle in the mild whirlpool, like horses on a merry-go-round, in the water that smelled of the mint that grew close by.

Or I ran to the barn where all you touched was warm. Grandpa's barn *was* bigger than his house. The doors had to be rolled back. It had a plank floor like a bridge that came to an end at the wall and another door. The barn was fuller of furnishings than the house, with barrels and tubs and crates and sacks piled on top of one another, odorous of all the different things they held. There was more to see, more to smell, more to climb on; nothing appeared to be forbidden. At times when the animals were down in the pasture, I could hear the dry seedcorn I let run through my fingers in the waiting stillness. After the animals had been led inside, now and then a horse's head would appear looking over the door of his stall. Then I played nearby, to give the head a chance to speak to me, like Falada the white horse's head nailed above the gate in the fairy tale. Falada says to the Goose Girl driving her geese, "Princess, Princess, passing by, / Alas, alas, if thy mother knew it, / Sadly, sadly her heart would rue it." Up in the loft, jumping wild in the new hay, I skinned through the hole in the floor, the way it went down when it was tossed to the trough below, and the trough caught me neatly. My brother Edward, not missing a jump overhead, didn't even know I'd gone.

There was an old buggy being used for hens to nest in, standing in the shadows of the barn. The shiny black buggy next to it, with a fringe on top, was the one in which Grandpa drove us to church. He allowed me to stand between his knees and hold the reins, even though I could not see over the horse's too-busy tail where we were going. But standing up on the back seat, I could see, squinting through the peephole window at the back, where the narrow wheels on a rainy Sunday sliced the road to chocolate ribbons. I got to hear Grandpa's voice on Sunday more than in all the rest of the week, because he sang in the choir; indeed, Grandpa led the choir.

At the end of the day at Grandpa's house, there wasn't much talking and no tales were told, even for the first time. Sometimes we all sat listening to a music box play.

There was a rack pulled out from inside the music box; we could see it holding shining metal discs as large as silver waiters, with teeth around the edges, and pierced with tiny holes in the shape of triangles or stars, like the tissue-paper patterns by which my mother cut out cloth for my dresses. When the discs began to turn, taking hold by their little teeth, a strange, chimelike music came about.

Its sounds had no kinship with those of "His Master's

Voice" that we could listen to at home. They were thin and metallic, not exactly keeping to time—rather as if the spoons in the spoonholder had started a quiet fretting among themselves. Whatever song it was was slow and halting and remote, as if the music box were playing something I knew as well as "Believe Me If All Those Endearing Young Charms" but did not intend me to recognize. It seemed to be reaching the parlor from far away. It might even have been the sound going through the rooms and up and down the stairs of our house in Jackson at night while all of us were here in Ohio, too far from home even to hear the clock striking from the downstairs hall. While we listened, there at the open window, the moonflowers opened little by little, and the song continued like a wire spring allowing itself slowly, slowly to uncoil, then just stopped trying. Music and moonflower might have been geared to move together.

Then, in my father's grown-up presence, I could not imagine him as a child in this house, the sober way he looked in the little daguerreotype, motherless in his fair bangs and heavy little shoes, sitting on one foot. Now I look back, or listen back, in the same desire to imagine, and it seems possible that the sound of that sparse music, so faint and unearthly to my childhood ears, was the sound he'd had to speak to him in all that country silence among so many elders where he was the only child. To me it was a sound of unspeakable loneliness that I did not know how to run away from. I was there in its company, watching the moonflower open.

• • •

I never saw until after he was dead a small keepsake book given to my father in his early childhood. On one page was a message of one sentence written to him by his mother on April 15, 1886. The date is the day of her death. "My dearest Webbie: I want you to be a good boy and to meet me in heaven. Your loving Mother." Webb was his middle name—her maiden name. She always called him by it. He was seven years old, her only child.

He had other messages in his little book to keep and read over to himself. "May your life, though short, be pleasant / As a warm and melting day" is from "Dr. Armstrong," and as it follows his mother's message may have been entered on the same day. Another entry reads: "Dear Webbie, If God send thee a cross, take it up willingly and follow Him. If it be light, slight it not. If it be heavy, murmur not. After the cross is the crown. Your aunt, Nina Welty." This is dated earlier—he was then three years old. The cover of the little book is red and embossed with baby ducklings falling out of a basket entwined with morning glories. It is very rubbed and worn. It had been given to him to keep and he had kept it; he had brought it among his possessions to Mississippi when he married; my mother had put it away.

In the farmhouse, the staircase was not in sight until evening prayers were over—it was time to go to bed then, and a door in the kitchen wall was opened and there were the stairs, as if kept put away in a closet. They went up like a ladder, steep and narrow, that we climbed on the way to bed. Step by step became visible as I reached it, by the climbing yellow light of the oil lamp that Grandpa himself carried behind me.

Back on Congress Street, when my father unlocked the door of our closed-up, waiting house, I rushed ahead into the air-less hall and stormed up the stairs, pounding the carpet of each step with both hands ahead of me, and putting my face right down into the cloud of the dear dust of our long absence. I was welcoming ourselves back. Doing likewise, more methodically, my father was going from room to room re-starting all the clocks.

I think now, in looking back on these summer trips— this one and a number later, made in the car and on the train—that another element in them must have been influencing my mind. The trips were wholes unto themselves. They were stories. Not only in form, but in their taking on direction, movement, development, change. They changed something in my life: each trip made its particular revela-tion, though I could not have found words for it. But with the passage of time, I could look back on them and see them bringing me news, discoveries, premonitions, promises— I still can; they still do. When I did begin to write, the short story was a shape that had already formed itself and stood waiting in the back of my mind. Nor is it surprising to me that when I made my first attempt at a novel, I entered its world—that of the mysterious Yazoo-Mississippi Delta—as a child riding there on a train: "From the warm window sill the endless fields glowed like a hearth in firelight, and Laura, looking out, leaning on her elbows with her head between her hands, felt what an arriver in a land feels—that slow hard pounding in the breast."

The events in our lives happen in a sequence in time, but in their significance to ourselves they find their own order, a timetable not necessarily—perhaps not possibly—chronological. The time as we know it subjectively is often the chronology that stories and novels follow: it is the continuous thread of revelation.

III

Finding a Voice

I had the window seat. Beside me, my father checked the progress of our train by moving his finger down the timetable and springing open his pocket watch. He explained to me what the position of the arms of the semaphore meant; before we were to pass through a switch we would watch the signal lights change. Along our track, the mileposts could be read; he read them. Right on time by Daddy's watch, the next town sprang into view, and just as quickly was gone.

Side by side and separately, we each lost ourselves in the experience of not missing anything, of seeing everything, of knowing each time what the blows of the whistle meant. But of course it was not the same experience: what was new to me, not older than ten, was a landmark to him. My father knew our way mile by mile; by day or by night, he knew where we were. Everything that changed under our eyes, in the flying countryside, was the known world to him, the imagination to me. Each in our own way, we hungered for all of this: my father and I were in no other respect or situation so congenial.

In Daddy's leather grip was his traveler's drinking cup, collapsible; a lid to fit over it had a ring to carry it by; it traveled in a round leather box. This treasure would be brought out at my request, for me to bear to the water cooler at the end of the Pullman car, fill to the brim, and bear back to my seat, to drink water over its smooth lip. The taste of silver could almost be relied on to shock your teeth.

After dinner in the sparkling dining car, my father and I walked back to the open-air observation platform at the end of the train and sat on the folding chairs placed at the railing. We watched the sparks we made fly behind us into the night. Fast as our speed was, it gave us time enough to see the rose-red cinders turn to ash, each one, and disappear from sight. Sometimes a house far back in the empty hills showed a light no bigger than a star. The sleeping countryside seemed itself to open a way through for our passage, then close again behind us.

The swaying porter would be making ready our berths for the night, pulling the shade down just so, drawing the green fishnet hammock across the window so the clothes you took off could ride along beside you, turning down the tight-made bed, standing up the two snowy pillows as high as they were wide, switching on the eye of the reading lamp, starting the tiny electric fan—you suddenly saw its blades turn into gauze and heard its insect murmur; and drawing across it all the pair of thick green theaterlike curtains— billowing, smelling of cigar smoke—between which you would crawl or dive headfirst to button them together with yourself inside, to be seen no more that night.

Finding a Voice

When you lay enclosed and enwrapped, your head on a pillow parallel to the track, the rhythm of the rail clicks pressed closer to your body as if it might be your heart beating, but the sound of the engine seemed to come from farther away than when it carried you in daylight. The whistle was almost too far away to be heard, its sound wavering back from the engine over the roofs of the cars. What you listened for was the different sound that ran under you when your own car crossed on a trestle, then another sound on an iron bridge; a low or a high bridge—each had its pitch, or drumbeat, for your car.

Riding in the sleeper rhythmically lulled me and waked me. From time to time, waked suddenly, I raised my window shade and looked out at my own strip of the night. Sometimes there was unexpected moonlight out there. Sometimes the perfect shadow of our train, with our car, with me invisibly included, ran deep below, crossing a river with us by the light of the moon. Sometimes the encroaching walls of mountains woke me by clapping at my ears. The tunnels made the train's passage resound like the "loud" pedal of a piano, a roar that seemed to last as long as a giant's temper tantrum.

But my father put it all into the frame of regularity, predictability, that was his fatherly gift in the course of our journey. I saw it going by, the outside world, in a flash. I dreamed over what I could see as it passed, as well as over what I couldn't. Part of the dream was what lay beyond, where the path wandered off through the pasture, the red clay road climbed and went over the hill or made a turn and was hidden in trees, or toward a river whose bridge I could see but whose name I'd never know. A house back at its distance at night showing a light from an open doorway, the morning faces of the children who stopped still in what they were doing, perhaps picking blackberries or wild plums, and watched us go by—I never saw with the thought of their continuing to be there just the same after we were out of sight. For now, and for a long while to come, I was proceeding in fantasy.

I learned much later—after he was dead, in fact, the time when we so often learn fundamental things about our parents—how well indeed he knew the journey, and how he happened to do so. He fell in love with my mother, and she with him, in West Virginia when she was a teacher in the mountain schools near her home and he was a young man from Ohio who'd gone over to West Virginia to work in the office of a lumber construction company. When they decided to marry, they saw it as part of the adventure of starting a new life to go to a place far away and new to both of them, and that turned out to be Jackson, Mississippi. From rural Ohio and rural West Virginia, that must have seemed, in 1904, as far away as Bangkok might possibly seem to young people today. My father went down and got a job in a new insurance company being formed in Jackson. This was the Lamar Life. He was promoted almost at once, made secretary and one of the directors, and he was to stay with the company for the rest of his life. He set about first thing finding a house in Jackson, then a town of six or eight thousand people, for them to live in until they could build a house of their own. So during the engagement, he went the thousand miles to see her when he could afford it. The rest of the time—every day, sometimes twice a day—the two of them sent letters back and forth by this same train.

Their letters had all been kept by that great keeper, my mother; they were in one of the trunks in the attic—the trunk that used to go on the train with us to West Virginia and Ohio on summer trips. I didn't in the end feel like a trespasser when I came to open the letters: they brought my parents before me for the first time as young, as inexperienced, consumed with the strength of their hopes and desires, as *living* on these letters. I would have known my mother's voice in her letters anywhere. But I wouldn't have so quickly known my father's. Annihilating those miles between them—the miles I came along to travel with him, that first time on the train—those miles he knew nearly altogether by heart, he wrote more often than any once a day, and mailed his letters directly onto the mail car—letters that are so ardent, so direct and tender in expression, so urgent, that they seemed to bare, along with his love, the rest of his whole life to me.

On the train I saw that world passing my window. It was when I came to see it was *I* who was passing that my self-centered childhood was over. But it was not until I began to write, as I seriously did only when I reached my twenties, that I found the world out there revealing, because (as with my father now) *memory* had become attached to seeing, love had added itself to discovery, and because I recognized in my own continuing longing to keep going, the need I carried inside myself to know—the apprehension, first, and then the passion, to connect myself to it. Through travel I first became aware of the outside world; it was through travel that I found my own introspective way into becoming a part of it.

This is, of course, simply saying that the outside world is the vital component of my inner life. My work, in the terms in which I see it, is as dearly matched to the world as its secret sharer. My imagination takes its strength and guides its direction from what I see and hear and learn and feel and remember of my living world. But I was to learn slowly that both these worlds, outer and inner, were different from what they seemed to me in the beginning.

The best college in the state was very possibly the private liberal-arts one right here in Jackson, but I was filled with desire to go somewhere away and enter a school I'd never passed on the street. My parents thought that I was too young at sixteen to live for my first year too far from home. Mississippi State College for Women was well enough accredited and two hundred miles to the north.

There I landed in a world to itself, and indeed it was all new to me. It was surging with twelve hundred girls. They came from every nook and corner of the state, from the Delta, the piney woods, the Gulf Coast, the black prairie, the red clay hills, and Jackson—as the capital city and the only sizeable town, a region to itself. All were clearly differentiated sections, at that time, and though we were all put into uniforms of navy blue so as to unify us, it could have been told by the girls' accents, by their bearings, the way they came into the classroom and the way they ate, where they'd grown up. This was my first chance to learn what the body of us were like and what differences in background, persuasion of mind, and resources of character there were among Mississippians—at that, among only half of us, for we were all white. I missed the significance of both what was in, and what was out of, our well-enclosed but vibrantly alive society. What was never there was money enough provided by our Legislature for education, and what was always there was a faculty accomplishing that education as a *feat*. Mississippi State College for Women, the oldest institution of its kind in America, poverty-stricken, enormously overcrowded, keeping within the tradition we were all used to in Mississippi, was conscientiously and, on the average, well taught by a dedicated faculty remaining and growing old there.

It was life in a crowd. We'd fight to get our mail in the basement post office, on rainy mornings, surrounded by other girls doing the Three Graces, where the gym teacher would have had to bring her first-period class indoors to practice. Even a gym piano, in competition with girls screaming over their letters and opening the food packages from home, was almost defeated. When we all had to crowd into compulsory chapel, one or two little frail undernourished students would faint sometimes—we had a fifteen-minute long Alma Mater to sing.

Old Main, the dormitory where I lived, had been built in 1860. It was packed to the roof with freshmen, three, four, or a half-dozen sometimes to the room, rising up four steep flights of wooden stairs. The chapel clock striking the hour very close by would shake our beds under us. It was the practice to use the fire escape to go to class, and at night to slip outside for a few minutes before going to bed.

It was the iron standpipe kind of fire escape, with a tin chute running down through it—all corkscrew turns from top to bottom, with holes along its passage where girls at fire drill could pour out of the different floors, and a hole at the bottom to pitch you out onto the ground, head still whirling.

It seemed impossible to be alone. Only music students had a good way. On a spring night you might hear one of them alone in a practice room of the Music Building, playing her heart out at an open window. It would be something like "Pale Hands I Loved Beside the Shalimar (Where Are You Now?)"—she'd be imagining of course that what she sent floating in the air was from someone else singing this song to *her*. At other times, when some strange song with low guttural notes and dragging movement, dramatically working up to a crescendo, was heard later still through that same open window, we freshmen told one another that was Miss Pohl, the spectacular gym teacher with the flying gray hair, who was, we had heard and believed, a Russian by birth, who'd been crossed, long years ago, in love. She may have indeed been crossed in love, but she was a Mississippian, just like us.

A time could be seized, close to bedtime, when it was possible to slip down the fire escape and, before the doors were all locked against my getting back, walk to an iron fountain on the campus and around it, with poetry running through my head. I'd bought the first book for my shelf from the college bookstore, *In April Once*, by William Alexander Percy, our chief Mississippi poet. Its first poem was one written from New York City, entitled "Home."

> *I have a need of silence and of stars.*
> *Too much is said too loudly. I am dazed.*
> *The silken sound of whirled infinity*
> *Is lost in voices shouting to be heard . . .*

Where I walked at that moment, within the little town of Columbus, and further within the iron gates of the campus of a girls' college at night, now everywhere going to bed, and while I said the poem to myself, around me was nothing *but* silence and stars. This did not impinge upon my longing. In the beautiful spring night, I was dedicated to *wanting* a beautiful spring night. To be *transported* to it was what

I wanted. Whatever a poem was about—that it could be called "Home" didn't matter—it was about somewhere else, somewhere distant and far.

I was lucky enough to have found for myself, at the very beginning, an outside shell, that of freshman reporter on our college newspaper, *The Spectator*. I became a wit and humorist of the parochial kind, and the amount I was able to show off in print must have been a great comfort to me. (I saw *The Bat* and wrote "The Gnat," laid in MSCW. The Gnat assumes the disguise of our gym uniform—navy blue serge one-piece with pleated bloomers reaching below the knee, and white tennis shoes—and enters through the College Library, after hours; our librarian starts screaming at his opening line, "Beulah Culbertson, I have come for those fines.") I'd been a devoted reader of S. J. Perelman, Corey Ford, and other humorists who appeared in *Judge* magazine, and I'd imagined that with these as a springboard, I could swim.

After great floods struck the state and Columbus had been overflowed by the Tombigbee River, I contributed an editorial to *The Spectator* for its April Fools issue. This lamented that five of our freshman class got drowned when the waters rose, but by this Act of God, it went on, there was that much more room now for the rest of us. Years later, a Columbus newspaperman, on whose press our paper was printed, told me that H. L. Mencken had picked up this chirp out of me for *The American Mercury* as sample thinking from the Bible Belt. But by chance, in the home of a town student, I had just met my first intellectual. Within a few moments he had lent me *Candide*! It was just published, the first Modern Library book (I believe the very first)—that thin little book with leatherlike covers that heated up, while you read, warmer than your hand. Voltaire, too, I could call on.

But I learned my vital lesson in the classroom.

Mr. Lawrence Painter, the only man teacher in the college, spent his life conducting the MSCW girls in their sophomore year through English Survey, from "Summer is y-comen in" to "I have a rendezvous with Death." In my time a handsome, learned, sandy-haired man—wildly popular, of course, on campus—he got instant silence when he would throw open the book and begin to read aloud to us.

In high-school freshman English, we had committed to memory "Whan that Aprille with his shoures soote . . ." which as poetry was not less remote to our ears than "Arma virumque cano . . ." I had come unprepared for the immediacy of poetry.

I felt the shock closest to this a year later at the University of Wisconsin when I walked into my art class and saw, in place of the bowl of fruit and the glass bottle and ginger jar of the still life I used to draw at MSCW, a live human being. As we sat at our easels, a model, a young woman, lightly dropped her robe and stood, before us and a little above us, holding herself perfectly contained, in her full self and naked. Often that year in Survey Course, as Mr. Painter read, poetry came into the room where we could see it and all around it, free-standing poetry. As we listened, Mr. Painter's, too, was a life class.

After I transferred, in my junior year, to the University of Wisconsin, I made in this far, new place a discovery for myself that has fed my life ever since. I express a little of my experience in a story, one fairly recent and not yet completed. It's the story of a middle-aged man who'd come from a farm in the Middle West, who's taciturn and unhappy as a teacher of linguistics and now has reached a critical point in his life. The scene is New Orleans; he and a woman are walking at night (they are really saying goodbye) and he speaks of himself without reserve to her for the first time.

He'd put himself through the University of Wisconsin, he tells her:

"And I happened to discover Yeats, reading through some of the stacks in the library. I read the early and then the later poems all in the same one afternoon, standing up, by the window . . . I read 'Sailing to Byzantium,' standing up in the stacks, read it by the light of falling snow. It seemed to me that if I could stir, if I could move to take the next step, I could go out into the poem the way I could go out into that snow. That it would be falling on my shoulders. That it would pelt me on its way down— that I could move in it, live in it—that I could die in it, maybe. So after that I had to *learn* it," he said. "And I told myself that I would. That I accepted the invitation."

Finding a Voice

The experience I describe in the story had indeed been my own, snow and all; the poem that smote me first was "The Song of Wandering Aengus"; it was the poem that turned up, fifteen years or so later, in my stories of *The Golden Apples* and runs all through that book.

At length too, at Wisconsin, I learned the word for the nature of what I had come upon in reading Yeats. Mr. Ricardo Quintana lecturing to his class on Swift and Donne used it in its true meaning and import. The word is *passion*.

It was my mother who emotionally and imaginatively supported me in my wish to become a writer. It was my father who gave me the first dictionary of my own, a Webster's Collegiate, inscribed on the flyleaf with my full name (he always included Alice, my middle name, after his mother) and the date, 1925. I still consult it. It was also he who expressed his reservations that I wouldn't achieve financial success by becoming a writer, a sensible fear; nevertheless he fitted me out with my first typewriter, my little red Royal Portable, which I carried off to the University of Wisconsin. It was also he who advised me, after I'd told him I still meant to try writing, even though I didn't expect to sell my stories to *The Saturday Evening Post* which paid well, to go ahead and try myself—but to prepare to earn my living some other way. My supportive parents had already very willingly agreed that I go farther from home for my last two years of college and sent me to Wisconsin—my father's choice for its high liberal-arts reputation. Now that I'd been graduated from there, they sent me to my first choice of a place to prepare for a job: New York City, at Columbia University Graduate School of Business. (As certain as I was of wanting to be a writer, I was certain of *not* wanting to be a teacher. I lacked the instructing turn of mind, the selflessness, the patience for teaching, and I had the unreasoning feeling that I'd be trapped. The odd thing is that when I did come to write my stories, the longest list of my characters turns out to be schoolteachers. They are to a great extent my heroines.)

My father did not bring it up, but of course I knew that he had another reason to worry about my decision to write. Though he was a reader, he was not a lover of fiction, because fiction is not true, and for that flaw it was forever inferior to fact. If reading fiction was a waste of time, so was the writing of it. (Why is it, I wonder, that humor didn't count? Wodehouse, for one, whom both of us loved, was a flawless fiction writer.)

But I was not to be in time to show him what I could do, to hear what he thought, on the evidence, of where I was headed.

My father had given immense study to the erection of the new Lamar Life home office building on Capitol Street, which was completed in 1925—"Jackson's first skyscraper." It is a delicately imposing Gothic building of white marble, thirteen stories high with a clock tower at the top. It had been designed, as my father had asked of the Fort Worth architect, to be congenial with the Episcopal parish church that stood next door to it and with the fine Governor's Mansion that faced it from across the street. The architect pleased him with his gargoyles: the stone decorations of the main entrance took the form of alligators, which related it as well to Mississippi.

At every stage of the building, Daddy took his family to see as much as we could climb over, usually on Sunday mornings. At last we could climb by the fire escape to reach the top. We stood on the roof, with the not-yet-working clock towering at our backs, and viewed all Jackson below, spread to its seeable limits, its green rim, where the still river-like Pearl River and the still-unpaved-over Town Creek meandered and joined together in their unmolested swamp, with "the country" beyond. We were located where we stood there—part of our own map.

At the grand opening, the whole of the new building was lighted from a top to bottom and the Company—its business now expanded into other Southern states—had a public reception. My father made a statement at the time: "Not a dollar was borrowed nor a security sold for the erection of this new building, and it is all paid for. The building will stand, now and always, free from all debt, as a most valuable asset to policy-holders."

It was a crowning year of his life. At the same time that the new building was going up, so was our new house, designed by the same architect. The house was on a slight hill (my mother never could see the hill) covered with its original forest pines, on a gravel road then a little out from town, and was built in a style very much of its day, of stucco and brick and beams in the Tudor style. We had moved in, and Mother was laying out the garden.

Six years later, my father was dead.

The Lamar Life tower is overshadowed now, and you can no longer read the time on its clocktower from all over town, as he'd wanted to be possible always, but the building's grace and good proportion contrast tellingly with the overpowering, sometimes brutal, character of some of the structures that rise above it. Renovators have sandblasted away the alligators that graced the entrance. But the Company still has its home there, and my father is remembered.

My father's enthusiasm for business was not the part of him that he passed on to his children. But his imaginative conception of the building, and his pride in seeing it go up and his love of working in his tenth-floor office with the windows open to the view on three sides, may well have entered into his son Edward. He went on to become an architect, especially gifted in design, who had a hand in a number of public buildings and private houses to be seen today in Jackson. Walter was a more literal kind of inheritor; after taking his master's degree in mathematics he went into the office of an insurance company—not the Lamar Life, but another.

Plans for the Company had included the launching of a radio station, and its office was a cubbyhole installed in the base of the tower. After my father was dead and the Great

Depression remained with us, I got a part-time job there. My first paid work was in communications: Mississippi's first radio station, operating there under the big clock, to which he would have given his nod of approval.

My first full-time job was rewarding to me in a way I could never have foreseen in those early days of my writing. I went to work for the state office of the Works Progress Administration as junior publicity agent. (This was of course one of President Roosevelt's national measures to combat the Great Depression.) Traveling over the whole of Mississippi, writing news stories for county papers, taking pictures, I saw my home state at close hand, really for the first time.

With the accretion of years, the hundreds of photographs—life as I found it, all unposed—constitute a record of that desolate period; but most of what I learned for myself came right at the time and directly out of the *taking* of the pictures. The camera was a hand-held auxiliary of wanting-to-know.

It had more than information and accuracy to teach me. I learned in the doing how *ready* I had to be. Life doesn't hold still. A good snapshot stopped a moment from running away. Photography taught me that to be able to capture transience, by being ready to click the shutter at the crucial moment, was the greatest need I had. Making pictures of people in all sorts of situations, I learned that every feeling waits upon its gesture; and I had to be prepared to recognize this moment when I saw it. These were things a story writer needed to know. And I felt the need to hold transient life in *words*—there's so much more of life that only words can convey—strongly enough to last me as long as I lived. The direction my mind took was a writer's direction from the start, not a photographer's, or a recorder's.

Along Mississippi roads you'd now and then see bottle trees; you'd see them alone or in crowds in the front yard of remote farmhouses. I photographed one—a bare crape myrtle tree with every branch of it ending in the mouth of a colored glass bottle—a blue Milk of Magnesia or an orange or green pop bottle; reflecting the light, flashing its colors in the sun, it stood as the centerpiece in a little thicket of peach trees in bloom. Later, I wrote a story called "Livvie" about youth and old age: the death of an old, proud, possessive man and the coming into flower, after dormant years, of his young wife—a spring story. Numbered among old Solomon's proud possessions is this bottle tree.

I know that the actual bottle tree, from the time of my actual sight of it, was the origin of my story. I know equally well that the bottle tree appearing in the story is a projection from my imagination; it isn't the real one except in that it is corrected by reality. The fictional eye sees in, through, and around what is really there. In "Livvie," old Solomon's bottle tree stands bright with dramatic significance, it stands vulnerable, ready for invading youth to sail a stone into the bottles and shatter them, as Livvie is claimed by love in the bursting light of spring. This I saw could be brought into being in the form of a story.

I was always my own teacher. The earliest story I kept a copy of was, I had thought, sophisticated, for I'd had the inspiration to lay it in Paris. I wrote it on my new typewriter, and its opening sentence was, "Monsieur Boule inserted a delicate dagger into Mademoiselle's left side and departed with a poised immediacy." I'm afraid it was a perfect example of what my father thought "fiction" mostly was. I was ten years older before I redeemed that in my first published story, "Death of a Traveling Salesman." I back-slid, for I found it hard to save myself from starting stories to show off what I could write.

In "Acrobats in a Park," though I laid the story in my home town, I was writing about Europeans, acrobats, adultery, and the Roman Catholic Church (seen from across the street), in all of which I was equally ignorant. In real life I fell easily under the spell of all traveling artists. En route to New Orleans, entertainments of many kinds would stop over in those days for a single performance in Jackson's Century Theatre. Galli-Curci came, so did Blackstone the Magician, so did Paderewski, so did *The Cat and the Canary* and the extravaganza *Chu Chin Chow*. Our family attended them all. My stories from the first drew visiting performers in, beginning modestly with a ladies' trio of the Redpath Chatauqua in "The Winds" and going so far as Segovia in "Music from Spain." Then, as now, my imagination was magnetized toward transient artists—toward the transience as much as the artists.

I must have seen "Acrobats in a Park" at the time I wrote the story as exotic, free of any experience as I knew it. And yet in the simplest way it isn't unrelated. The acrobats I led in procession into Smith Park in Jackson, Mississippi, were a *family*. They sat down in our family park, eating their lunch under a pin-oak tree I knew intimately. A father, a mother, and their children made up the troupe. At the center of the little story is the Zorros' act: the feat of erecting a structure of their bodies that holds together, interlocked, and stands like a wall, the Zorro Wall. Writing about the family act, I was writing about the family itself, its strength as a unit, testing its frailty under stress. I treated it in an artificial and oddly formal way; the stronghold of the family is put on public view as a structure built each night; on the night before the story opens, the Wall has come down when the most vulnerable member slips, and the act is done for. But from various points within it and from outside it, I've been writing about the structure of the family in stories and novels ever since. In spite of my unpromising approach to it, my fundamental story form might have been trying to announce itself to me.

My first good story began spontaneously, in a remark repeated to me by a traveling man—our neighbor—to whom it had been spoken while he was on a trip into North Mississippi: "He's gone to borry some fire." The words, which carried such lyrical and mythological and dramatic overtones, were real and actual—their hearer repeated them to me.

As usual, I began writing from a distance, but "Death of a Traveling Salesman" led me closer. It drew me toward what was at the center of it, to a cabin back in the red clay hills— perhaps just such a house as I used to see from far off on a train at night, with the firelight or lamplight showing yellow from its open doorway. In writing the story I approached and went inside with my traveling salesman, and had him, pressed by imminent death, figure out what was there:

> Bowman could not speak. He was shocked with know-ing what was really in this house. A marriage, a fruit-ful marriage. That simple thing. Anyone could have had that.

Writing "Death of a Traveling Salesman" opened my eyes. And I had received the shock of having touched, for the first time, on my real subject: human relationships. Daydream-ing had started me on the way; but story writing, once I was truly in its grip, took me and shook me awake.

My temperament and my instinct had told me alike that the author, who writes at his own emergency, remains and needs to remain at his private remove. I wished to be, not effaced, but invisible—actually a powerful position. Perspective, the line of vision, the frame of vision—these set a distance.

An early story called "A Memory" is a discovery in the making. This is how it begins:

One summer morning when I was a child I lay on the sand after swimming in the small lake in the park. The sun beat down—it was almost noon. The water shone like steel, motionless except for the feathery curl behind a distant swimmer. From my position I was looking at a rectangle brightly lit, actually glaring at me, with sun, sand, water, a little pavilion, a few solitary people in fixed attitudes, and around it all a border of dark rounded oak trees, like the engraved thunderclouds surrounding illustrations in the Bible. Ever since I had begun taking painting lessons, I had made small frames with my fingers, to look out at everything.

Since this was a weekday morning, the only persons who were at liberty to be in the park were either children, who had nothing to occupy them, or those older people whose lives are obscure, irregular, and consciously of no worth to anything: this I put down as my observation at that time. I was at an age when I formed a judgment upon every person and every event which came under my eye, although I was easily frightened. When a person, or a happening, seemed to me not in keeping with my opinion, or even my hope or expectation, I was terrified by a vision of abandonment and wildness which tore my heart with a kind of sorrow. My father and mother, who believed that I saw nothing in the world which was not strictly coaxed into place like a vine on our garden trellis to be presented to my eyes, would have been badly concerned if they had guessed how often the weak and inferior and strangely turned examples of what was to come showed themselves to me.

I do not know even now what it was that I was waiting to see; but in those days I was convinced that I almost saw it at every turn. To watch everything about me I regarded grimly and possessively as a *need*. All through this summer I had lain on the sand beside the small lake, with my hands squared over my eyes, finger tips touching, looking out by this device to see everything: which appeared as a kind of projection. It did not matter to me what I looked at; from any observation I would conclude that a secret of life had been revealed to me—for I was obsessed with notions about concealment, and from the smallest gesture of a stranger I would wrest what was to me a communication or a presentiment.

This is not, on reaching its end, an observer's story. The tableau discovered through the young girl's framing hands is unwelcome realism. How can she accommodate the existence of this view to the dream of love, which she carried already inside her? Amorphous and tender, from now on it will have to remain hidden, her own secret imagining. The frame only raises the question of the vision. It has something of my own dreaming at the train window. But now the dreamer has stopped to look. After that, dreaming or awake, she will be drawn in.

"A Still Moment"—another early story—was a fantasy, in which the separate interior visions guiding three highly individual and widely differing men marvelously meet and converge upon the same single exterior object. All my characters were actual persons who had lived at the same time, who would have been strangers to one another, but whose lives had actually taken them at some point to the same neighborhood. The scene was in the Mississippi wilderness in the historic year 1811—"*anno mirabilis*," the year the stars fell on Alabama and lemmings, or squirrels perhaps, rushed straight down the continent and plunged into the Gulf of Mexico, and an earthquake made the Mississippi River run backwards and New Madrid, Missouri, tumbled in and disappeared. My real characters were Lorenzo Dow the New England evangelist, Murrell the outlaw bandit and murderer on the Natchez Trace, and Audubon the painter; and the exterior object on which they all at the same moment set their eyes is a small heron, feeding.

I never wrote another such story as that, but other sorts of vision, dream, illusion, hallucination, obsession, and that most wonderful interior vision which is memory, have all gone to make up my stories, to form and to project them, to impel them.

The frame through which I viewed the world changed

too, with time. Greater than scene, I came to see, is situation. Greater than situation is implication. Greater than all of these is a single, entire human being, who will never be confined in any frame.

Writing a story or a novel is one way of discovering *sequence* in experience, of stumbling upon cause and effect in the happenings of a writer's own life. This has been the case with me. Connections slowly emerge. Like distant landmarks you are approaching, cause and effect begin to align themselves, draw closer together. Experiences too indefinite of outline in themselves to be recognized for themselves connect and are identified as a larger shape. And suddenly a light is thrown back, as when your train makes a curve, showing that there has been a mountain of meaning rising behind you on the way you've come, is rising there still, proven now through retrospect.

It seems to me, writing of my parents now in my seventies, that I see continuities in their lives that weren't visible to me when they were living. Even at the times that have left me my most vivid memories of them, there were connections between them that escaped me. Could it be because I can better see their lives—or any lives I know—today because I'm a fiction writer? See them not as fiction, certainly—see them, perhaps, as even greater mysteries than I knew. Writing fiction has developed in me an abiding respect for the unknown in a human lifetime and a sense of where to look for the threads, how to follow, how to connect, find in the thick of the tangle what clear line persists. The strands are all there: to the memory nothing is ever really lost.

The little keepsake book given to my father so long ago, of which I never heard a word spoken by anybody, has grown in eloquence to me. The messages that were meant to "go with him"—and which did—the farewell from his mother on the day of her death; and the doctor's following words that the child's own life would be short; the admonition from his Aunt Penina to bear his cross and murmur not—made a sum that he had been left to ponder over from the time he had learned to read. It seems to me that my father's choosing life insurance as his work, and indeed he exhausted his life for it, must have always had a deeper reason behind it than his conviction, strong as it was, in which he joined the majority in the twenties, that success in business was the solution to most of the problems of living—security of the family, their ongoing comfort and welfare, and especially the certainty of education for the children. This was partly why the past had no interest for him. He saw life in terms of the future, and he worked to provide that future for his children.

Right along with the energetic practice of optimism, and deeper than this, was an abiding awareness of mortality itself—most of all the mortality of a parent. This care, this caution, that ruled his life in the family, and in the business he chose and succeeded in expanding so far, began very possibly when he was seven years old, when his mother, asking him with perhaps literally her last words to be a good boy and meet her in heaven, died and left him alone.

Strangely enough, what Ned Andrews had extolled too, in all his rhetoric, was the future works of man and the leaving of the past behind. No two characters could have been wider apart than those of Ned Andrews and Christian Welty, or more different in their self-expression. They never knew each other, and the only thing they had in common was my mother's love. Who knows but that this ambition for the betterment of mankind in the attainable future was the quality in them both that she loved first? She would have responded to the ardency of their beliefs. I'm not sure she succeeded in having faith in their predictions. Neither got to live their lives out; the hurt she felt in this was part of her love for both.

My father of course liberally insured his own life for the future provision of his family, and had cause to believe that all was safe ahead. Then the Great Depression arrived. And in 1931 a disease that up to then even he had never heard of, leukemia, caused his death in a matter of weeks, at the age of fifty-two.

I believe the guiding emotion in my mother's life was pity. It encompassed the world. During the war (World War II), she heard on a radio broadcast that the Chinese, fearing their great library would be destroyed, took the books up in their hands and put them onto their backs and carried all of them,

123

on foot, over long mountain paths, away to safety. Mother cried for them, and for their books. Almost more than eventual disaster, brave hope that it could be averted undid her. She had had so many of those brave hopes herself. Crying for the old Chinese scholars carrying their precious books over the mountain gave her a way too of crying for herself, with her youngest child, who was serving with the Navy at the battle of Okinawa.

She suffered perhaps more than an ordinary number of blows in her long life. We her children, like our father before us, had to learn the lesson that we never would be able to console her for any of them; especially could we not console her for what happened to ourselves.

Her strongest habit of thought was association. There is no way to help that.

When my father was dying in the hospital, there was a desperate last decision to try a blood transfusion. How much was known about compatibility of blood types then, or about the procedure itself, I'm unable to say. All I know is that there was no question in my mother's mind as to who the donor was to be.

I was present when it was done; my two brothers were in school. Both my parents were lying on cots, my father had been brought in on one and my mother lay on the other. Then a tube was simply run from her arm to his.

My father, I believe, was unconscious. My mother was looking at him. I could see her fervent face: there was no doubt as to what she was thinking. This time, *she* would save *his* life, as he'd saved hers so long ago, when she was dying of septicemia. What he'd done for her in giving her the champagne, she would be able to do for him now in giving him her own blood.

All at once his face turned dusky red all over. The doctor made a disparaging sound with his lips, the kind a woman knitting makes when she drops a stitch. What the doctor meant by it was that my father had died.

My mother never recovered emotionally. Though she lived for over thirty years more, and suffered other bitter losses, she never stopped blaming herself. She saw this as her failure to save his life.

As the New York train pulled, close to midnight, out of the station at home, your friends stood waving as though they'd never see you again. Your last view of Jackson from your window was an old dark wooden building by the tracks topped by a hand-painted sign under an arc light: "Where Will YOU Spend Eternity?" This sign was also the first thing you saw in the dawn when the train brought you back home again.

As the train picked up speed, rolled faster out of town, I would lie back with an iron cage around my chest of guilt.

In the later times of the Depression, I saved all I could from my part-time or temporary jobs in Jackson to go to New York. I hoped to show my stories and the photographs I'd taken over Mississippi in the Depression to an editor who would like them—either or both—enough to publish them. A two-week stay in the City, which I'd proved could be managed for $100 then—and that included the theatre—seemed long enough to me for a decision; but I would have to come away without knowing. It didn't at all occur to me how many times over my own manuscripts were multiplied on an editor's desk. It was the *encouraging* responses that took so long to come—a year sometimes; the editors who gave me an extraordinary amount of understanding and hope, and praise too, had so far found they still had to say no in the end. All this would go on the train with me, up there and back. It was part of my flying landscape.

I knew that even as I was moving farther away from Jackson, my mother was already writing to me at her desk, telling me she missed me but only wanted what was best for me. She would not leave the house till she had my wire, sent from Penn Station the third day from now, that I had arrived safely. I was not to worry about her or things at home, about how she was getting along. She anxiously awaited my letter after I had tried my stories on the publishers.

I knew this was how she must have waited when my father had left on one of his business trips, and I thought I could guess how he, the train lover, the trip lover, must have felt too while he remained away. I thought of the big box of Fanny May Chocolates he brought back from Chicago, the sheet music to "I Want to Be Happy" from *No, No, Nanette* that would tell us all about the show he'd so much enjoyed and wished we had seen with him. Taking trips tore all of us up inside, for they seemed, each journey away from home, something that might have been less selfishly undertaken, or something that would test us, or something that had better be momentous, to justify such a leap into the dark. The torment and guilt—the torment of having the loved one go, the guilt of being the loved one gone—comes into my fiction as it did and does into my life. And most of all the guilt then was because it was true: I had left to arrive at some future and secret joy, at what was unknown, and what was now in New York, waiting to be discovered. My joy was connected with writing; that was as much as I knew.

In Meridian (I had only gone ninety miles from Jackson) there was a wait of hours for the train that went from New Orleans to New York. The ceiling lights in the station were so lofty that you couldn't see to read. Long after midnight, the first signal came from the blackness outside—the whistle blowing for the curve south of town. The ancient and familiar figure of the black lady who for the last two hours had carried around coffee in a black iron pot as large as a churn would be at your side as you woke up. She was the sole attendant. Now she proceeded to call the stations. Her white frilled bonnet and starched white apron only made her look official at 2 A.M. in Meridian. She shouted out the whole list of destinations exactly as she must have done for fifty years under the echoing vault of the grand railroad station of its day. Above the thunder of the approaching engine, and then a bell heard ringing, rising in pitch as it rang nearer, and its alarm right at our ears now, and over the clanging and banging of arrival at the platform and the shriek of vented steam, one human voice recited the roster of our destination. Slowly and from deep-down inside her each name came measured out to us like words in a church: "Birmingham ... Chattanooga ... Bristol ... Lynchburg ... Washington ... Baltimore ... Philadelphia ... and New York." And changing herself one more time—now into the porter—she would start loading her arms and shoulders with all our suitcases, as many as she could carry at one time, and herd us down the platform to our daycoach, getting rid of us herself to make sure we were gone. She appears as herself in one story I wrote, "The Demonstrators," but she's there in spirit in many more. She was to me the very Angel of Departure, and I thought how often, parked over there insensible in the sleeping car waiting for the same connection, in those earlier times, I'd slept through her.

The trip to New York meant two nights and parts of three days sitting up and changing trains several times. This cost only $17.50 each way, cheaper if I could run into an excursion rate out of Washington. We spent all one day crossing the width of Tennessee, then peacefully rural. I came to know the layout of any given town we went through, the name of the hardware store, where to look for a bank clock that kept good time. I knew where the shade patches came at mid-afternoon in upland pastures, and remembered to look for the pony among the horses gathered there. The same little dogs from summer to summer would always chase our train past the gates of certain farms. We went through the mountains by night; you could only hear your passage, not see. If I were asleep and a stop awakened me at dawn, I'd look out the window instinctively knowing I'd see the station where the fat, simple-minded boy would be skipping down the sidewalk at the drugstore corner, just in time to greet the train. I could have prophesied I'd see the same man and woman standing on ladders every time we went around a certain long curve, endlessly re-painting their greenhouse.

Yet those were the last years when there seemed to be timetables, schedules, in operation. With the approach of the War, on crowded and ill-maintained trains, the kind never running on time and often breaking down, the route itself retraced the same country as in those earlier days; landmarks were slower then to fade away. But the train often stopped for no discernible reason in the open country and stood without sound or motion, like a becalmed ship. My father would have been right out there, finding out the trouble from the brakeman or the engineer, taking out his watch, as concerned as they were. You had to expect to stop dead where the track reached a three-way meeting of branchlines in perfectly empty country; a tiny shed-like station carried the name "Ooltewah." Was this "Waterloo" said backwards? But nothing, it seemed to me, ever did happen at this prolonged stop. We met no other train; no train came to pass us. Destination, when the train isn't moving, seems only a forgotten dream.

Once, when my train came to one of those inexplicable stops in open country, this happened: Out there was spread around us a long, high valley, a green peaceful stretch of Tennessee with distant farmhouses and, threading off toward planted fields, a little foot path. It was sunset. Presently, without a word, a soldier sitting opposite me rose and stepped off the halted train. He hadn't spoken to anybody for the whole day and now, taking nothing with him and not stopping to put on his cap, he just left us. We saw him walking right away from the track, into the green valley, making a long shadow and never looking back. The train in time proceeded, and as we left him back there in the landscape, I felt *us* going out of sight for *him*, diminishing and soon to be forgotten.

Eventually, without stirring a mile from home, I fell into the safest possible hands. After I had written enough stories that were the best I could make them, my future literary agent Diarmuid Russell and my future editors, who became my friends for life, found *me*. (John Woodburn, an editor who came through Jackson scouting for his publisher, wrote when he'd persuaded the house to take my first book, "I knew when I tasted your mother's waffles everything would turn out all right.")

Travel itself is part of some longer continuity.

Just this past summer, in some effects of my father's, I

130

came across photographic negatives I'd never seen—even their size was different from all those he made of our family. I had them printed and found before me scenes of unfamiliar places—city streets and buildings and tram cars and docksides, public parks with running children who seemed in costume; young ladies sitting in boats or strolling in long skirts and straw hats; ships, flags, stretches of sea or some wide river—and all at once Niagara Falls, no mistake about that, by day and by night, lit up. On the other hand, there was a frozen waterfall with a man in overcoat and hat posing beside it, holding to one long icicle as to a lady's hand in an opera-length white glove. I was mystified until at a later time this same summer I ran across by chance a railway timetable with ferry-boat schedules and hours for band concerts, and excursion prices from Halifax, for a given week in August, 1903. That was my father's, all right—he would have taken every one of those offers. And the date I recognized now as the summer before the year he married my mother. In those snapshots I was looking at the festival scenes of his last fling.

No, I was looking at more than that. It came back to me that my mother had said he'd offered her a choice between the Thousand Islands and Jackson, Mississippi, as their future home, and she'd chosen Jackson, Mississippi; we had her to thank. But I could see now that of course he would have gone up there to look over the Thousand Islands and ridden the train or sailed the St. Lawrence from Ontario to Halifax, stopping off for Niagara Falls, and taken those pictures to bring her, before he'd say a rash thing like that to Chessie Andrews. And here they were, the choice she didn't take. She'd chosen the other place, and here was I now, one of the results, in it, with pictures of the other choice now turning up in my hand.

Along with the ferry timetable and the schedule of excursions and the souvenir book of the Thousand Islands, I came across a sizeable commercial photograph taken of my father. A slim figure in a light business suit, he is standing, with one foot up on a rock, apparently right in the rapids of Niagara Falls. His usual expression of kind regard is on his face. He'd probably had this trick photograph made just to present to my mother. It made me remember what countless times he tried by joking means to make her laugh. When he did, it took *him* with delighted surprise, too—a triumph for both of them. I could imagine her being handed this picture of her fiancé standing in the rapids above Niagara Falls with his hat in his hand, and saying to him, "I don't see the humor in that." He *knew* how terrified she was of the water!

What discoveries I've made in the course of writing stories all begin with the particular, never the general. They are mostly hindsight: arrows that I now find I myself have left behind me, which have shown me some right, or wrong, way I have come. What one story may have pointed out to me is of no avail in the writing of another. But "avail" is not what I want; freedom ahead is what each story promises—

beginning anew. And all the while, as further hindsight has told me, certain patterns in my work repeat themselves without my realizing. There would be no way to know this, for during the writing of any single story, there is no other existing. Each writer must find out for himself, I imagine, on what strange basis he lives with his own stories.

I had been writing a number of stories, more or less one after the other, before it belatedly dawned on me that some of the characters in one story were, and had been all the time, the same characters who had appeared already in another story. Only I'd written about them originally under different names, at different periods in their lives, in situations not yet interlocking but ready for it. They touched on every side. These stories were all related (and the fact was buried in their inceptions) by the strongest ties—identities, kinships, relationships, or affinities already known or remembered or foreshadowed. From story to story, connections between the characters' lives, through their motives or actions, sometimes their dreams, already existed: there to be found. Now the whole assembly—some of it still in the future—fell, by stages, into place in one location already evoked, which I saw now was a focusing point for all the stories. What had drawn the characters together there was one strong strand in them all: they lived in one way or another in a dream or in romantic aspiration, or under an illusion of what their lives were coming to, about the meaning of their (now) related lives.

The stories were connected most provocatively of all to

me, perhaps, through the entry into my story-telling mind of another sort of tie—a shadowing of Greek mythological figures, gods and heroes that wander in various guises, at various times, in and out, emblems of the characters' heady dreams.

Writing these stories, which eventually appeared joined together in the book called *The Golden Apples*, was an experience in a writer's own discovery of affinities. In writing, as in life, the connections of all sorts of relationships and kinds lie in wait of discovery, and give out their signals to the Geiger counter of the charged imagination, once it is drawn into the right field.

The characters who go to make up my stories and novels are not portraits. Characters I invent along with the story that carries them. Attached to them are what I've borrowed, perhaps unconsciously, bit by bit, of persons I have seen or noticed or remembered in the flesh—a cast of countenance here, a manner of walking there, that jump to the visualizing mind when a story is underway. (Elizabeth Bowen said, "Physical detail cannot be invented." It can only be chosen.) I don't write by invasion into the life of a real person: my own sense of privacy is too strong for that; and I also know instinctively that living people to whom you are close—those known to you in ways too deep, too overflowing, ever to be plumbed outside love—do not yield to, could never fit into, the demands of a story. On the other hand, what I do make my stories out of is the *whole* fund of my feelings, my responses to the real experiences of my own life, to the rela-

134

tionships that formed and changed it, that I have given most of myself to, and so learned my way toward a dramatic counterpart. Characters take on life sometimes by luck, but I suspect it is when you can write most entirely out of yourself, inside the skin, heart, mind, and soul of a person who is not yourself, that a character becomes in his own right another human being on the page.

It was not my intention—it never was—to invent a character who should speak for me, the author, in person. A character is in a story to fill a role there, and the character's life along with its expression of life is defined by that surrounding—indeed is created by his own story. Yet, it seems to me now, years after I wrote *The Golden Apples*, that I did bring forth a character with whom I came to feel oddly in touch. This is Miss Eckhart, a woman who has come from away to give piano lessons to the young of Morgana. She is formidable and eccentric in the eyes of everyone, is scarcely accepted in the town. But she persisted with me, as she persisted in spite of herself with the other characters in the stories.

Where did the character of Miss Eckhart come from? There was my own real-life piano teacher, "eligible" to the extent that she swatted my hands at the keyboard with a flyswatter if I made a mistake; and when she wrote "Practice" on my page of sheet music she made her "P" as Miss Eckhart did—a cat's face with a long tail. She did indeed hold a recital of her pupils every June that was a fair model for Miss Eckhart's, and of many another as well, I suppose. But the character of Miss Eckhart was miles away from that of the teacher I knew as a child, or from that of anybody I did know. Nor was she like other teacher-characters I was responsible for: my stories and novels suddenly appear to me to be full of teachers, with Miss Eckhart different from them all.

What the story "June Recital" most acutely shows the reader lies in her inner life. I haven't the slightest idea what my real teacher's life was like inside. But I knew what Miss Eckhart's was, for it protruded itself well enough into the story.

As I looked longer and longer for the origins of this passionate and strange character, at last I realized that Miss Eckhart came from me. There wasn't any resemblance in her outward identity: I am not musical, not a teacher, nor foreign in birth; not humorless or ridiculed or missing out in love; nor have I yet let the world around me slip from my recognition. But none of that counts. What counts is only what lies at the solitary core. She derived from what I already knew for myself, even felt I had always known. What I have put into her is my passion for my own life work, my own art. Exposing yourself to risk is a truth Miss Eckhart and I had in common. What animates and possesses me is what drives Miss Eckhart, the love of her art and the love of giving it, the desire to give it until there is no more left. Even in the small and literal way, what I had done in assembling and connecting all the stories in *The Golden Apples*, and bringing them off as one, was not too unlike the June recital itself.

Not in Miss Eckhart as she stands solidly and almost

opaquely in the surround of her story, but in the making of her character out of my most inward and most deeply feeling self, I would say I have found my voice in my fiction.

Of course any writer is in part all of his characters. How otherwise would they be known to him, occur to him, become what they are? I was also part Cassie in that same story, the girl who hung back, and indeed part of most of the main characters in the connected stories into whose minds I go. Except for Virgie, the heroine. She is right outside me. She is powerfully like Miss Eckhart, her co-equal in stubborn and passionate feeling, while more expressive of it—but fully apart from me. And as Miss Eckhart's powers shrink and fade away, the young Virgie grows up more rampant, and struggles into some sort of life independent from all the rest.

If somewhere in its course your work seems to you to have come into a life of its own, and you can stand back from it and leave it be, you are looking then at your subject—so I feel. This is how I came to regard the character of Virgie in *The Golden Apples*. She comes into her own in the last of the stories, "The Wanderers." Passionate, recalcitrant, stubbornly undefeated by failure or hurt or disgrace or bereavement, all the while heedlessly wasting of her gifts, she knows to the last that there is a world that remains out there, a world living and mysterious, and that she is of it.

Inasmuch as Miss Eckhart might have been said to come from me, the author, Virgie, at her moments, might have always been my subject.

• • •

Through learning at my later date things I hadn't known, or had escaped or possibly feared realizing, about my parents—and myself—I glimpse our whole family life as if it were freed of that clock time which spaces us apart so inhibitingly, divides young and old, keeps our living through the same experiences at separate distances.

It is our inward journey that leads us through time—forward or back, seldom in a straight line, most often spiraling. Each of us is moving, changing, with respect to others. As we discover, we remember; remembering, we discover; and most intensely do we experience this when our separate journeys converge. Our living experience at those meeting points is one of the charged dramatic fields of fiction.

I'm prepared now to use the wonderful word *confluence*, which of itself exists as a reality and a symbol in one. It is the only kind of symbol that for me as a writer has any weight, testifying to the pattern, one of the chief patterns, of human experience.

Here I am leading to the last scenes in my novel, *The Optimist's Daughter*:

> She had slept in the chair, like a passenger who had come on an emergency journey in a train. But she had rested deeply.
>
> She had dreamed that she *was* a passenger, and riding with Phil. They had ridden together over a long bridge.

Awake, she recognized it: it was a dream of something that had really happened. When she and Phil were coming down from Chicago to Mount Salus to be married in the Presbyterian Church, they came on the train. Laurel, when she travelled back and forth between Mount Salus and Chicago, had always taken the sleeper. She and Phil followed the route on the day train, and she saw it for the first time.

When they were climbing the long approach to a bridge after leaving Cairo, rising slowly higher until they rode above the tops of bare trees, she looked down and saw the pale light widening and the river bottoms opening out, and then the water appearing, reflecting the low, early sun. There were two rivers. Here was where they came together. This was the confluence of the waters, the Ohio and the Mississippi.

They were looking down from a great elevation and all they saw was at the point of coming together, the bare trees marching in from the horizon, the rivers moving into one, and as he touched her arm she looked up with him and saw the long, ragged, pencil-faint line of birds within the crystal of the zenith, flying in a V of their own, following the same course down. All they could see was sky, water, birds, light, and confluence. It was the whole morning world.

And they themselves were a part of the confluence. Their own joint act of faith had brought them here at the very moment and matched its occurrence, and proceeded as it proceeded. Direction itself was made beautiful, momentous. They were riding as one with it, right up front. It's our turn! she'd thought exultantly. And we're going to live forever.

Left bodiless and graveless of a death made of water and fire in a year long gone, Phil could still tell her of her life. For her life, any life, she had to believe, was nothing but the continuity of its love.

She believed it just as she believed that the confluence of the waters was still happening at Cairo. It would be there the same as it ever was when she went flying over it today on her way back—out of sight, for her, this time, thousands of feet below, but with nothing in between except thin air.

Of course the greatest confluence of all is that which makes up the human memory—the individual human memory. My own is the treasure most dearly regarded by me, in my life and in my work as a writer. Here time, also, is subject to confluence. The memory is a living thing—it too is in transit. But during its moment, all that is remembered joins, and lives—the old and the young, the past and the present, the living and the dead.

As you have seen, I am a writer who came of a sheltered life. A sheltered life can be a daring life as well. For all serious daring starts from within.

Acknowledgments

The origin of this book is the set of three lectures delivered at Harvard University in April, 1983, to inaugurate the William E. Massey lecture series. I am deeply grateful to Harvard University and to the graduate program in the History of American Civilization at whose invitation I wrote and gave the lectures. Mr. David Herbert Donald, of this program, gave me the best of his firm guidance and understanding. I am grateful to Mrs. Aida D. Donald, executive editor of Harvard University Press, for her kindness and patient care during their preparation in present form. To Mr. Daniel Aaron, whose suggestion as to the direction and course the lectures might take strongly encouraged me in their writing, I wish to express particular gratitude.

Jackson, Mississippi, 1983